AUTOGRAPH

Carolina Soul
THE DOWN HOME TASTE OF THE CAROLINAS

PROSPERITY PUBLICATIONS, LLC
San Antonio, TX
www.prosperitypublications.com

www.cookwithrome.com

Copyright, January, 10th 2020: Chef Jerome Brown
All rights reserved.

No part of this book may be reproduced in any form or by any means without the prior written consent of the publisher, excepting brief quotes used in review.

ISBN: 978-0-9995674-0-1

Layout: Pixel Munki, LLC

Foreword

Wow... Delectable flavors dancing all in your mouth. These dishes you will experience are not just Southern....they are more like a part of you, your experiences and the love and passion comes alive in each dish. Thank you for asking me to share in this great project and I'm sure others will discover what we receive when we get together and that's "PURE MAGIC WITH LOVE POURING OUT!"

GINA NEELY
Food Network host, New York Times best selling author

Acknowledgements

GOD IS EVERYTHING! Without him, I would be lost without a cause. I'm thankful to him for this journey and for this tremendous gift that he is allowing me to share with the world. It's all to him I owe.

Joshua, God truly smiled on me when he blessed us with you. My son, I couldn't be prouder of you than I already am. You have overcome your own odds to be where you are now. I couldn't have asked for a better son. I love you!

Jasmine, you never cease to amaze me. The young lady that you continue to develop into is amazing to see. Your competitive spirit will always take you where you want to go. The two of you are going to be great doctors.

To my cousins, and extended family, there's far too many of you to name. I love you all. I know I don't cook for you all when I come around but that's because, you can all hold your own in the kitchen. At least most of you. I'm not sure about you Dumar and Lisa Speight. LOL!

To Donia and Terri, thank you for allowing me to crash at your place when I'm at home. You are a tremendous blessing to the family. Dakari's meatloaf is going to be amazing.

To Bruce and Tina. Thank you for allowing your home to be a place the family can come and just be ourselves. You are appreciated. Whenever I'm there, I always feel the love.

That's how we were taught, and that's how we were raised. Unfortunately, not every family can say this.

To Ursula and Simone. Thanks for being a blessing and enriching my life more than you will ever know. You two were the official taste testers for the book. Ursula, even though you cook extremely well, stop changing my recipes.

JR, you are a God send. I don't know what I would do without you. Every time I've called you, you've answered with a yes. I appreciate you from the bottom of my heart. Your touch on "Eat Like A Celebrity" and now, "Carolina Soul," I know I have a winner.

Thank you, thank you, thank you!

To Prosperity Publications; You took a chance on me, and for this I'm forever grateful. I'm excited about this book and the future projects that we will forge together.

To Dr. Lanetta Bronte'. Where do I began? I owe you a debt of gratitude. When others thought they were a better choice, you stuck with me and took a chance. Thank you to say the least. The Foundation for Sickle Cell Disease Research is not only impacting the lives of millions, but you are a true gift to every community. Whatever your future holds, I want you to know that you are a shero in my book forever. I pray continued happiness in your life forever.

To Lindsey and Letty. You are two of my favorite people. Lindsey, thank you for keeping the haters in line. Don't get rid of them all. I need to keep some around. It lets me know, I'm doing something right.

To Chef Sondra' Rhodes, Chef Ricky Simpson, and Chef Tony Moore, you three need to get back to work. No shout outs. LOL! The three of you have saved my ass on so many occasions. Where would I be without you? I'm thankful for you guys for always having my back. I can't pay you enough and thank you just doesn't seem adequate. I love you guys and I thank your wives for signing your permission slips and letting you out the house.

To Jesonya Whitfield, Pastor Kim, Tunda Wannamaker, Kim McCrakin, and Wanda Parker. Where would I be without your prayers. You ladies are what I call the "A-Team". This is who I call to get a prayer through when mine don't seem to be working. LOL

Last but certainly not least, to my siblings Gwendale, Ken, Bonita, Linda, Amanda, Beth, and Tricia, Lethia, and Judy. I love you all. My life wouldn't be complete if any one of you were not a part of it.

Fatimah and Gina, I can't settle the dispute. You're both my favorite along with the rest of my cousins. So, cut it out. LOL

Note From Rome

Would you believe it? For some reason I didn't think I had it in me to write another cookbook. While giving much thought to what I would write about specifically, I began to reflect on the things I love most dearly. One of those things, or in this case, one of those places is the Carolinas.

North Carolina will always be home to me. Even though I was born in New Jersey, my mother was a Carolina girl through and through. So, I guess one could say I got it honestly.

As I travel all over the world, I seem to consistently meet people who have heard a lot of wonderful things about the Carolinas but have never traveled here. That's why I named the book "Carolina Soul." I want to introduce to some and present to others a lot of the hidden gems that make these two great states so special. It is my desire to tempt your palate to experience the down-home taste that keeps me coming back for more, and around the table.

Thank you for taking this journey with me. I appreciate every one of you for taking the time to see and taste the Carolinas through the lens in which I see it.

Bon appetit!

While giving much thought to
what I would write about specifically, I
began to reflect on the things I love most dearly.
One of those things, or in this case,
ONE OF THOSE PLACES IS THE CAROLINAS.

Table of Contents

1	WELCOME TO CAROLINA
9	ROSEMARY CREAM CORN
10	CORN, TOMATOES & OKRA
11	SAUTÉED KALE
14	NORTH CAROLINA SKEWERED PORK TENDERLOIN
15	SPICED HOT WATER CORN BREAD
19	NORTH CAROLINA SHE CRAB SOUP
21	SWEET POTATO CHEESE CAKE WITH COGNAC PECAN SAUCE
24	SISTA' ANNIE BRUCE'S BISCUITS
25	COLLARD GREEN EMPANADAS
26	CREAMED PEAS & MUSHROOMS
28	"GOOD OLE" COUNTRY OXTAILS & GRITS
30	MAPLE & GARLIC ROASTED PORK BELLY
32	NORTH CAROLINA CHOPPED BBQ
35	BLACKEYE PEA & SAUSAGE SOUP
36	MUSSELS & COUSCOUS SALAD
37	ROME'S COLESLAW
40	AUNT BETTE'S BBQ NECK BONE
42	BRAISED BEEF SHORT RIBS
43	ROME'S SWEET POTATO CORN BREAD
46	UNCLE LARRY'S SWEET HUSHPUPPIES
48	TATER JACK TURNOVERS
50	GRILLED PORK CHOPS BATHED IN PEPSI MUSCADINE REDUCTION
51	BOILED PEANUTS
53	BLACKEYE PEAS & OKRA
54	BOUDIN STUFFED QUAIL
57	AUNT BESSIE'S CAROLINA CORN PUDDING
60	WEEZY'S LUMP CRAB AND PASTA
62	BROWN SUGAR GLAZED PORK CHOPS
64	OLD SCHOOL BEANIES AND WEENIES
65	NECK BONES & RICE

66	MARSALA MEATLOAF
67	BULLHEAD CATFISH STEW
68	CAROLINA SHRIMP BOIL
70	GARLIC & CHEDDAR SHRIMP AND GRITS
74	SWEET GULLAH OYSTER & SAUSAGE CORNBREAD DRESSING
77	RUSSELL'S BEER BATTERED FROG LEGS
78	CREOLE MAYONNAISE
78	CAROLINA REMOULADE SAUCE
80	RON'S COLLARDS AND CABBAGE
81	GOLDEN FRIED SPOTS
84	GREAT NORTHERN CAROLINA CHILI
86	SOUTH CAROLINA BBQ SAUCE
88	CHARLESTON RED RICE
91	KATHERINE'S BOILED CHICKEN AND NOODLES
92	SOUTHERN VEGGIE BITES
95	PAN FRIED GRIT CAKES
97	SAUTÉED BRUSSELS SPROUTS TOSSED IN GARLIC BUTTER GLAZE
100	CHEF ROME'S CAROLINA STYLE FRENCH TOAST FINISHED WITH D'USSE COGNAC SYRUP
101	JAMAICAN OXTAIL STEW
102	JASMINE SAFFRON COCONUT RICE
104	THE DIRTIEST RICE
106	FRIED GREEN TOMATO PO BOY WITH CRAWFISH REMOULADE
110	QUAN'S RIBS
111	MAMMA'S BABY LIMA AND SHRIMP
112	LINGUINI AND BAY SCALLOPS TOSSED IN LEMON BUTTER SAUCE
116	WILD BERRY SKILLET
117	GRILLED RED DRUM
118	OPEN FACE BOLOGNA & EGG SANDWICH
119	BAKED CREAMY CAULIFLOWER
120	CRAB STUFFED DEVILED EGGS
121	POTATO & LEEK SOUP
122	GRILLED VEGETABLE & QUINOA SALAD
124	LOBSTER ENCHILADAS
126	BANANA LESS PUDDING

127	FIVE CHEESE & PORK BELLY MAC
128	MOMMA'S SWEET POTATO PIE
129	"THAT" SALMON RECIPE
131	MOW THE LAWN
132	ADULT HOT CHOCOLATE
135	SUNNY LICKS
136	THE "G" SPOT
139	SKILLET POTATOES
143	CARROT AND SWEET POTATO BISQUE
145	SMOKED GOUDA AND KALE EMPANADAS
147	HONEY MUSTARD GLAZED SALMON
148	THE GREAT NORTHERN SOUP
151	SAUTÉED LIVER FIESTA
152	SPINACH AND CHEDDAR QUICHE
154	DRUNKEN FRUIT COCKTAIL
155	SMOOTHIE SUNRISE
156	CARROT, APPLE AND PEAR SMOOTHIE
156	TROPICAL POPSICLE DELIGHT
157	PINEAPPLE RUM GLAZED CHICKEN BREAST
158	WILD BERRY PARFAIT TOPPED WITH HOMEMADE GRANOLA
160	SOUTHWESTERN QUINOA SALAD
161	SPICY CRAB STUFFED AVOCADO
162	CREAMY APPLE & PEAR DRESSING
163	SUNNY OJ POACHED CARROTS
168	CREAMY PEANUT BUTTER PIE
169	THREE BEAN ENCHILADAS
172	VEGETARIAN GUMBO
174	CREAM OF CHICKEN GUMBO
177	SOUTHWESTERN CHICKEN DEVILED EGG
178	SEAFOOD SPAGHETTI
184	WAKANDA STEW *(AFRICAN PEANUT STEW)* WAKANDA
188	RICE PUDDING *(BLACK RICE PUDDING)*

Welcome to Carolina

When I'm in the Carolinas I enjoy visiting various cities for not only the unique local culture but the cuisine as well. The Carolinas have beaches on one end, mountains on the other. There are world class medical facilities such as Duke Medical, UNC's woman's hospital and the Medical university of South Carolina. Some of the best college sports teams are located in the Carolinas. Duke, UNC Chapel Hill, University of South Carolina Gamecocks and the Clemson tigers are all Carolina namesakes. The Carolinas are also home to some of the top HBCU's in the nation. My daughter spends all of my money at the historical HBCU North Carolina A&T where she attends college. LOL!

The Carolinas is the birthplace to America's blessing known as Pepsi! New Bern, NC is the birthplace of the original Pepsi name called "Brad's Drink," in 1893 by Caleb Bradham. Pepsi is still the number one drink in my book. You can always hear stories of the "older folk" talk about how they would "knock off work," after toiling the field and would sit on the front porch and enjoy a nice cold Pepsi with some peanuts at the bottom. Pepsi, a true Carolina tradition!

The Carolinas has also produced some of the world's best athletes. The Carolina's have major sports teams such as the Carolina Panthers. From superstar basketball player Alex English from Columbia, SC to Michael Jordan from North Carolina and A'ja Wilson Amercia's sweetheart and one of the most amazing young basketball players ever! Our athletes have made us proud. Gospel music icons Pastor Shirley Caesar, Luther Barnes and Thomas L. Culture are all products of the Carolinas.

The Carolinas are a beautiful melting pot of people from all nations, cultures, socio-economic statuses but they love their food! Carolinians have made tremendous strides in technology and medicine that affects the entire world. Raleigh remains in the top 10 places for conducting business in the United States. If you're ever in Raleigh and are looking for great food, I promise you it won't be very hard to find.

My list of top 10 restaurants alone will keep you busy for a while. Some of my personal favorites are "42nd St Oyster Bar & Grill," "Firebirds Wood Fired Grill," "Saint Jacques French Cuisine," "The Cowfish Sushi Burger Bar," and "Champa Thai & Sushi Restaurant" located in Brier Creek. The Saki lemon drop is amazing.

I discovered the Brier Creek Beer Garden a few years ago. It reminds me that North Carolina also features some of the most outstanding beers that I've ever tasted anywhere. From the "Brewgaloo" craft beer festival to the historic Rural Hill and of course the Jolly skull beer & wine festival, NC knows beer! In fact, I can't forget about the World Beer Festival hosted in "Bull City" aka Durham which is becoming well known on the beer scene worldwide.

You can't mention beer in the Carolina's without mentioning the moonshine industry as well. If you remember the show "The Dukes of Hazzard" from the 1980's you are sure to "recollect" as my grandmother would say Uncle Jessie and his Kentucky moonshine. My cousin Speight calls it "stump hole," which is the Carolina name for "moonshine." Broadslab distillery over in Johnston county is the go to place for that good ole' authentic taste. If you ever visit Asheville be sure to check out the Biltmore Estate an amazing historical site, and the head on over to Cherokee NC to see the native American reenactment of "Unto these Hills' which chronicles the Native American trail of tears. When I visit Asheville as a treat for myself I always stop at the Howling Moon Distillery. From the apple pie, peach, and strawberry moonshine flavors to the 150-year-old mountain moonshine, you can't find better flavored moonshines anywhere else. I laugh when I think about moonshine because my uncles found many ways to create moonshine. Back in the day we would take a little bit of moonshine and add it to our tea to fight off colds. I don't know who came up with that remedy, but it worked. We would get under a blanket and let the cold sweat out of our bodies. Of course, there were the days of having a little too much moonshine in my eggnog during the holidays. North Carolina cities Raleigh, Durham, and Charlotte are the "hip" cities in NC. These cities have corporations, high tech industries, world class colleges and universities along with great food. There are lots of activities in these locales, which equates to there never being a dull moment. There's always an opportunity to meet new people from all over the world. From the annual Woman's empowerment conference in Raleigh to CIAA tournament every year in Charlotte, these cities never sleep. From day parties to after hour dip-ins, I will always have somewhere to go when I want to have a good time in North Carolina.

"Nothing can be finer than to be in Carolina," is an understatement when talking about South Carolina. I immensely enjoy the drive from my original point of origin whether it be Raleigh or Rocky Mount as I am headed to the SC coast. Myrtle Beach is one of my favorite cities to relax and have fun. Each summer I find myself at the North Beach Plantation resort preparing meals for some of my NBA clients and friends. The drive to Myrtle Beach is like taking a journey through a tour of history. The unique dives and hole in the wall restaurants sparks a sense of nostalgia for me. I always look forward to seeing the fresh picked watermelons being sold on the side of the road or the pickled things you can find in gas stations on Highway 378, 76, 501, and Interstate's 20 & 95 are incredible. There's nothing like those pop up farmers markets. Sometimes I pull over just to see what they have. I must say, I'm rarely disappointed with my findings. Often times when I was Raymond Felton's personal chef, I'd show up with a watermelon from one of those stands on the side of the road in the Latta, Mullins and Marion, SC area right off of highway 76. It didn't matter which one I'd pick, it was a winner. Someone told me a secret once. They said if you ever see a scratched-up watermelon, you're looking at a sweet watermelon. The animals are the ones who can pick them out. The raccoons or rabbits sense of smell will lead them to the right ones. They try to scratch the fruit to break it open to get to the inside which leaves scratch marks on the outer melon. Just follow the scratch mark and you will find a sweet melon. That little trick has never failed me. So much for the thumping. I didn't trust what I was listening for anyway, LOL!

Charleston is another phenomenal Carolina city that I enjoy as well. I will probably come back to Charleston again and again in this book. I can remember my first time there over three decades ago. It was an early morning, I can remember standing on the balcony of my hotel overlooking the ocean. A family of dolphins were circling in the ocean. I thought it was the coolest thing to see them in their natural habitat. Charleston to me is a very special place. As an African American, I am astutely aware that most blacks who were brought to the United States from Africa came through the port of Charleston. The history, the richness, the "magic" coupled with the beautiful natural habitats makes Charleston one of the best cities in the country. The cuisine in Charleston is superb, from crab, to oysters, scallops, this city produces some of the best seafood worldwide. Unlike a lot of beach towns that may only serve hot dogs, burgers and deli sandwiches, Charleston has so many wonderful restaurants with enough options for the many palates that travel there from all over the world.

I am so excited that I found a new SC gem. I had the opportunity to visit the thriving capital of Columbia, SC this past winter. This is an amazing city that is home to The University of South Carolina, and two historical HBCU institutions Benedict College and Allen University along with three other colleges. Columbia is home to Fort Jackson, the largest army training post. As a former Army cook it gives me pride to always see a town that welcomes soldiers and their families. Columbia is a world class city full of arts, culture, Riverbank Zoo and I hear the mayor Stephen Benjamin is quite the chef as well. I will have to plan a trip back to Columbia to engage with the Honorable Mayor over a grill or a stove. It was surprising to discover that the Marvel character "Luke Cage," whose real name is Mike Colter hails from Columbia, SC and studied at Benedict college. Go Tigers!

I had the opportunity to spend the day at Heathwood Hall Episcopal school in Columbia,

SC with my Goddaughter India. I felt almost "forced" to make the trip after she kept mentioning her "cooking team" and how excited she was about a cooking competition that her school participated in. She was relentless about picking my brain about cooking tips, the purpose of food presentation, etc. etc. I could hear the elation in her voice. Her excitement is what made me visit the city that I had only frequented as a layover on flights in the past. So, when a kid is so excited about something, we as adults get excited as well. But, as a Chef, you want to taste everything to see what the hype is about since she bragged about Heathwood's dining hall. India was 100% on point! The food at Heathwood was to die for! Chef Jim, Chef Mac and their team not only have a carving station, superb entrees but the food was a mixture of elegance, southern cuisine, spices that were not stifled but they also provided a myriad of healthy selections as well, that would put any five star restaurant to shame! You ready for this? Heathwood is for early childhood up to 12th grade students! No wonder they received an award for their dining facility. Those kids eat better than many of the celebrities I have worked for from the King of Sweden, Priscilla Presley, Nancy Kerrigan, and even Shaq! Hands down, the food at Heathwood Hall Episcopal school is the best "school food," I have ever eaten! I have interacted with many schools from elementary thru college in a number of capacities from teaching, doing cooking demonstrations, judging competitions and mentoring all over the world. However, the experience, the hospitality, not just the amazing food at Heathwood Hall was none that I have ever experienced. The therapeutic atmosphere nestled on the beautiful quaint campus was incredible! Good food coupled with good people is hard to find these days!

Go Highlanders!

The upstate area of SC is a pristine part of SC that is full of beautiful foliage, mountainous terrain and southern hospitality. Cities in the upstate have much to offer, Greenville has an amazing, robust night life and local restaurants. Spartanburg, SC is home of BMW which is proof that the Carolinas have a lot to offer in every diaspora including manufacturing and corporations. Anderson, SC another upstate city is home to Chadwick Boseman, star of the Marvel movie, "Black Panther." #WakandaForever!

There is a little town tucked away in the Upstate called Gaffney, SC. The first thing you see when you enter the town is huge Peach which serves as a water tower. Of course as a Chef I am always looking for food and I was not disappointed. There is this little spot called "The Clock," which I believe God reached down from heaven and made the fried green tomatoes himself! They have entrees that take me back to my childhood such as fried bologna, with the bubble in the middle.

Gaffney is the peach capital of the Carolinas. (I heard it through the grapevine that SC produces more peaches than Georgia, but you didn't hear it from me) To discuss peaches is akin to Bubba Gump discussing shrimp in the movie Forrest Gump.

White peaches, sugar peaches, big peaches all things peaches that melt in your mouth like cotton candy that will send you into a sugar overload. Yum! I have never seen such a "peach site," in my life. Peach bbq sauce, peach jam, peach chow chow, peach cider! A little birdie told me that a Gaffney trip is not complete until you attend one of Dr. Carol McFadden's "get together's for a southern bbq and/or bash. Gaffney is home to the Hamrick's store headquarters and the Tanger outlet is a "big deal" in Gaffney. Just a few short miles away you can enjoy a live reenactment of the "Battle of Cowpens," one of the most important battles of the American Revolutionary war.

I can't help it but I keep going back to Charleston! There's a restaurant in Charleston called "The Glass Onion." They have a fried green tomato po boy that is out of this world. This sandwich is massive, sinful and whether you are Catholic or not you will need to go to confession after eating one of these masterpieces. It is comprised of a perfect French bread, an excellent pimento cheese, garden fresh green tomatoes with a wonderful buttery crust. Low country cooking classics like this contribute to visitors coming back time and time again. It's the simple dishes that make the most impact when it comes to comfort food. The crab rice served at Hannibal's Kitchen in Charleston is a very simple dish but it boasts big time flavor. Always remember, less is more in the kitchen!

If you are an oxtail lover like me, hold onto your horses! Boy, oh boy do I have a place for you. Chaleston's "Addielee's restaurant" has some of the best oxtails in the country. It's stewed and served over a tomato based rice. I've enjoyed oxtails many ways. Of course, Jamaican style is also a favorite for many! But I love the approach to the way it's cooked by the South Carolinians. There's a combination of international flavors married with spices to create that big bold flavor that I love so much. When I'm home in Rocky Mount, North Carolina I like to drop in on one of my favorite places to eat called "Taste of paradise" and grab a large oxtail dinner or maybe the curried chicken. Home Run! If you're ever in Rocky Mount, drop on by and tell them I sent you.

South Carolina has it's own exquisite food taste and cuisine that is relative to the Palmetto state. From the annual "Chitterling strut," in Salley, SC to the elegant cuisine of the Low County, the palmetto state certainly stands out when it comes to food and festivals. Foods such as salmon croquettes, grits and gravy, pickled pigs feet are revered as delicacies. I would be remiss if I did not mention BBQ! BBQ in South Carolina is equally as revered as BBQ in North Carolina. SC is known for the mustard based bbq while NC has the vinegar based BBQ on lock.

Many of the slaves from Africa brought their own knowledge of utilizing herbs, spices and their special way of cooking which we still utilize today in many Carolinian dishes. Those recipes are a part of Southern Culture and the American diaspora. The Carolinas have everything anyone would ever want! Whether you are a Gamecock, Blue Devil, Clemson or Tarheel fan or you prefer to chill at the beautiful coastal beaches in either state you will always have something to do. Or, if you prefer to hang out in the Cape area, the mountainous artsy city of Asheville or the small city feel of a small college town such as Hartsville, SC. Whether your preference is to witness the beautiful historical experience of an HBCU homecoming coupled with tailgates, stepshows along with superb marching bands such as North Carolina A&T and SC State University or if your preference is the big city banking capital of Charlotte. Whether your preference is the sleepy tobacco town of Mullins, SC or the beautiful, historic town of Pembroke NC which is such a poignant reminder of our beautiful Native American culture to my amazing city of Rocky Mount, NC known as "the half way" point of I-95, the Carolinas has it all!

The Carolinas are a blend of all things that represent the best in America. Because collectively we have more that unites us that divides us.

I hope these recipes help you to discover your Inner Carolina Soul! *The Carolinian people, culture and food is truly the Soul of The United States!* **ENJOY! CHEF JEROME BROWN, CELEBRITY CHEF**

ROSEMARY CREAM CORN

COOK TIME: 40 MINUTES | SERVES: 4

Ingredients

3 Strips of bacon *(reserve the fat)*

½ Stick of sweet cream butter

8 large ears of corn *(use a paring knife to remove the corn from the husk)*

2 Teaspoons of fine chopped fresh rosemary

1 Tablespoons of sugar

2 Teaspoons of coarse black pepper

1 Teaspoon of salt

1 Cup of heavy cream

½ Cup of water

½ Cup of chopped scallions

Directions

Place a large skillet on the stove over medium high heat. Preheat the pan until it's hot. Place the bacon in the pan and cook until it's crispy. Remove the bacon from the pan and place on a paper towel to drain. Chop the bacon and set aside for garnish later.

Add the butter to the bacon fat. Once the butter is melted, add the corn, rosemary, sugar, pepper and salt. Mix well and cover. Stir the corn occasionally. Allow the corn to sauté for about 10 minutes. Add the cream and water. Reduce the heat to low. Cover and continue cooking for about 30 minutes. Place the corn into a serving bowl and top with chopped bacon and scallions. Enjoy!

CORN, TOMATOES & OKRA

COOK TIME: **20** MINUTES | SERVES: **4**

Ingredients

1 Stick of sweet cream butter

1 Tablespoon of olive oil

3 Ears of fresh corn *(Use a paring knife to remove the corn from the cob)*

4 Roma tomatoes *(diced)*

1 Small yellow onion *(small diced)*

1 Green bell pepper *(small diced)*

1 Tablespoon of minced garlic

1 Tablespoon of sugar

1 Teaspoon of dry oregano

1 Teaspoon of salt

1 Teaspoon of black pepper

1 Cup of cut okra

Directions

Place a large skillet on the stove on medium high. Add the butter and olive oil. Once the butter has melted, add the corn, tomatoes, onion, pepper, garlic, and sugar. Cover and reduce the heat. Allow to simmer on medium low for 15 minutes. Add the remaining ingredients and cover. Continue cooking for an additional 5 minutes. Serve immediately Enjoy!

Carolina Soul | 10

SAUTÉED KALE

COOK TIME: 2 MINUTES | SERVES: 2

Ingredients

3 Strips of bacon *(chopped)*

1 Small onion *(chopped)*

1 Tablespoon of minced garlic

Pinch of crushed red pepper flakes

2 Pounds of young kale *(stems and leaves coarsely chopped)*

½ Cup of vegetable or chicken stock

1 Teaspoon of seasoned salt

1 Teaspoon of black pepper

Directions

Cook the bacon, onion, garlic, and red pepper flakes in a large skillet or saucepan over medium high heat. Add kale, then sauté for about two minutes. Next, you will need to add the stock, salt and pepper. Cover and continue to cook for 2 minutes. Serve as a side. Enjoy!

NORTH CAROLINA SKEWERED PORK TENDERLOIN

COOK TIME: **15** MINUTES | SERVES: **4**

Ingredients

QUICK BBQ SAUCE

½ Cup of cider vinegar

½ Cup of white vinegar

1 Cup of ketchup

3 Tablespoons of white sugar

3 Tablespoons of brown sugar

Pinch of crushed red pepper

2 Tablespoons of water

¼ Cup of vegetable oil

PORK TENDERLOINS

1 ¼ pound of pork tenderloin
(cut into 1- inch cubes)

½ Cup of olive oil

2 Tablespoons of water

2 Tablespoons of vinegar

1 Tablespoon of minced garlic

1 Tablespoon of cracked black pepper

1 Tablespoon of seasoned salt

Zest of a half lime

Zest of a small tangerine

1 Tablespoon of seasoned salt

1 Tablespoon of rotisserie chicken seasoning

Directions

YOU WILL NEED 5 WOOD SKEWERS. Add 1 cup of bourbon to two cups of water. Place the skewers in the water to soak for at least 30 minutes until ready for use.

In a small sauce pot combine all the ingredients and mix well. Heat over medium low. Set aside for later use.

Combine all the ingredients in a bowl and mix well. Place the pork into the ingredients and toss well. Place in the refrigerator and marinate for about 30 minutes.

Preheat an outdoor grill over medium high heat. Use a non-stick spray to prevent the pork from sticking. Remove the pork from the refrigerator and evenly divide between the skewers. Place the skewers onto the grill. Close the grill and cook for about 5 minutes before turning. Brush the pork lightly with the BBQ sauce. Cook for about 15 minutes or desired doneness.

NOTE: *If you're using a meat thermometer, pork should be cooked to an internal temperature of 175 degrees Fahrenheit. Enjoy!*

Carolina Soul | 14

SPICED
HOT WATER CORN BREAD

COOK TIME: 4 - 5 MINUTES | SERVING MAY VARY

Ingredients

2 Cups of self-rising yellow cornmeal

2/4 Cups of cake flour

2 Teaspoons of salt

1 Tablespoon of sugar

1 Teaspoon of baking powder

1 Egg (beaten)

¼ Cup of jalapeno pepper (chopped)

½ Cup of whole kernel corn (frozen or canned)

¼ Cup of minced red bell pepper

2 Cups of boiling water

Vegetable shortening

Directions

In a stainless-steel bowl, mix together the cornmeal, flour, salt, sugar and baking powder. Mix well. Stir in the egg, jalapeno, corn, and bell pepper. Add the boiling water to the mix. Use a spoon to combine all the ingredients. Mix well. Place warm water in a separate bowl for your hands as mixture will be sticky.

Pour the oil in a cast iron skillet to a depth of about two inches and heat to 375 degrees.

Shape the cornmeal mixture into whatever your desired shape. Use the warm water to keep your hands clean between forming the patties or balls. You may also use a tablespoon as a measuring guide. Fry each in the hot oil, turning once, until crisp and golden brown all over. Cook for about 4-5 minutes. Drain on paper towels. Can be served with greens, beans, or stews. Enjoy!

She Crab Soup

Some say this soup originated from the COAST OF SOUTH CAROLINA, but hey, I'll take it no matter where it originated from.

SHE CRAB SOUP in the Carolinas is one of the most popular delicacies served in both states. As a crab connoisseur, I am always looking for ways to incorporate crab meat into my recipes. Whether on the Hatteras coast in North Carolina or the low county in South Carolina seafood is a way of life, a cultural icon and a favorite amongst Americans from all walks of life. Red snapper, king mackerel, speckled trout, flounder are just a few of the tastes from the ocean that are enjoyed by many. My horoscope is a cancer, so since I was born under the sign of the crab I wonder if that has anything to do with my love for seafood. The North Carolina She crab soup is truly one of my favorites. Some say this soup originated from the coast of South Carolina, but hey, I'll take it any way it comes. There's several varieties of this soup, however, the crab roe is what makes it "she crab." It's hard to get your hands on fresh roe, but well worth the effort if you are able to get your hands on some fresh roe. One thing's for sure, fresh she crabs reigns supreme.

NORTH CAROLINA
SHE CRAB SOUP

COOK TIME: **15** MINUTES | SERVES: **4**

Ingredients

1 Quart of half and half

2 Cups of crab or chicken broth *(low sodium)*

1 Cup of heavy cream

1 Stick of salted butter

½ Cup of all-purpose flour

½ Cup of fine chopped celery

½ Cup of fine chopped white onion

1 Tablespoon of minced garlic

1 Teaspoon of dry thyme

1 Teaspoon of white pepper

2 Teaspoons of Kosher salt

1 Tablespoon of Worcestershire sauce

1 Tablespoon of pepper sauce

1 ½ Pounds of Lump crab

½ Cup of sherry

1 Tablespoon of chopped chives for garnish

Directions

Place an 8-quart pot on the stove over medium low heat. Pour in the half and half, crab broth, and heavy cream. In the meantime, place a small skillet on the stove over medium high. Place the butter into the skillet. Allow the butter to melt. Add the flour to the butter and whisk until smooth and creamy. Remove the flour mixture and set aside for later use.

Turn the flame up to medium high on the cream mixture and allow it to come to a simmer. Add to the pot the celery, onion, garlic, thyme, pepper, salt, Worcestershire sauce and pepper sauce. Stir constantly. Continue to simmer for about 10 minutes. Turn the flame up and allow the mixture to come to a boil. Add the rue to the mix while stirring. Mix well.

Reduce the heat and allow the soup to continue to simmer. Add the crab and half the roe to the soup and stir. Spoon the soup into the bowls. Drizzle the sherry and remaining roe on top. Garnish with fresh chopped chives. Enjoy!

SWEET POTATO CHEESE CAKE
With COGNAC PECAN SAUCE

COOK TIME: 55 - 60 MINUTES | **SERVES:** 8

Ingredients

CRUST

1 ¼ Cups graham cracker crumbs

¼ Cup of sugar

¼ Cup of butter *(unsalted, melted)*

½ Teaspoon of ground mace

FILLING

1 Large sweet potato *(baked, mashed, and pureed')*

4 Packages of cream cheese *(softened)*

¼ Cup of sour cream

½ Cup of brown sugar *(firmly packed)*

1 Cup of sugar

4 Eggs

1 Teaspoon of cinnamon

1 Teaspoon of nutmeg

1 Teaspoon of vanilla

TOPPING

½ Stick of butter

1 Cup of Brown sugar

1 Cup of chopped pecans

2 Ounces of Cognac

Directions

Wash the potato and wrap in aluminum foil. Place the potato in a baking dish. Bake for one hour. Bake until the potato is fork tender. Allow the potato to cool completely. Place the potato into a blender and puree for about 5 seconds. Set aside until ready for use.

Preheat the oven to 300 degrees. In a mixing bowl combine the graham cracker crumbs, melted butter, sugar, and mace. Mix well.

Press the mixture into the bottom of a 10-inch spring form pan. Bake for 8 minutes. Remove from the oven and set aside.

Place the cream cheese and sour cream into a large mixing bowl. Using a hand mixer, blend until smooth and creamy. Add the two sugars and continue to mix on medium speed until well blended for about 30 seconds. Add the sweet potato mixture. Mix on low speed for about one minute. Scrap the sides of the bowl and continue to mix. Add one egg at a time and blend well after each egg. Add the cinnamon, nutmeg and vanilla. Beat on medium speed until incorporated for about 15 seconds.

Turn the oven up to 400 degrees. Pour the mixture into the spring form pan. Place the spring form pan into a larger pan with higher edges. Fill the larger pan with hot water to one third the height of the spring form pan and place it into the oven. Bake for about 1 hour and 30 minutes. Add hot water to the larger pan as needed. Bake until the center is set.

While the cheesecake is cooking, place a non-stick skillet onto the stove on medium high. Place the butter into the pan and allow the

Directions *(cont.)*

butter to melt. Add the brown sugar and combine with the butter until smooth. Add the pecans and mix well. Stir in the cognac. Allow the sauce to simmer for about one minute on medium low heat.

Remove the cheesecake from the oven once the center is set. Allow the cheesecake to cool to room temperature. If necessary, slightly warm the sauce so that it can pour easier. Pour the sauce over the cheesecake. Cover with wax paper until you're ready to remove from the pan. Place the cheesecake into the refrigerator for about 4 hours. Once you're ready to slice the cheesecake, unbuckle the pan. Use a paring knife if necessary to help loosen from the edges. Slice and serve with your favorite ice cream. Enjoy!

MY GRANDMOTHER'S NAME WAS ANNIE. HER CHURCH SISTERS CALLED HER "SISTA' ANNIE." In my debut cookbook "Eat Like a Celebrity," I mentioned that my grandparents had 23 children. I spent quite a lot of time with about 14 of my aunts and uncles. I can't remember a time whenever I visited North Carolina and didn't see a pan of those wonderful biscuits on the stove. Usually they were covered with a clean towel. There was nothing like the taste of molasses or honey with Grandma Annie's homemade biscuits. Often times the biscuits would be served with fried salt herring fish or fresh salmon croquettes. There was almost a ritualistic, magical experience the way Grandma Annie rolled the biscuits out. She would use an old with wooden rolling pin along with a stainless-steel biscuit cutter. That is such a poignant part of my life that I will never forget. The thought of grandma's biscuits will always spark up nostalgia in a way no other food can for me. It was a signature staple in the house. It was something you could always expect. I miss those days and Grandma Annie.

> There was almost a *ritualistic, magical experience* the way **GRANDMA ANNIE ROLLED THE BISCUITS OUT.**

SISTA' ANNIE BRUCE'S BISCUITS

COOK TIME: 15 MINUTES | SERVES: MAKES 12 BISCUITS

Ingredients

PREHEAT OVEN TO 425

2 Cups of Self-rising flour

1 Cup of cake flour

1 Tablespoon of sugar

1 Teaspoon of salt

1 Teaspoon of baking powder

¼ Cup of solid shortening

½ Cup of unsalted butter *(cold, cut into ¼ inch pieces)*

1 Cup of buttermilk

2 Sticks of melted butter

Directions

In a large bowl, whisk the flours, sugar, salt, and baking powder together. Add the shortening and butter. Use your hand to combine the shortening and butter into the dry ingredients until the mixture becomes coarse and gritty. Next, add the buttermilk then stir with a wooden spoon until all the dough is all mixed together.

Sprinkle the clean surface with enough flour to cover the area being used to roll out the dough. Add the dough to the surface and roll the biscuits out to about a 1/2 of an inch thick. Try to use a biscuit cutter if possible. Place the biscuits in a pan or cookie sheet about an inch apart. Place the biscuits into the refrigerator for about 30 minutes. Place the biscuits into the oven for about 15 mins: bake until golden brown. Brush with melted butter and serve immediately. Enjoy!

COLLARD GREEN EMPANADAS

COOK TIME: **15** MINUTES | SERVINGS: **2** EACH

Ingredients

COLLARD GREENS

1 Pound of fresh collard greens *(stem removed, washed well, chopped)*

1 Small white onion *(minced)*

4 Cloves of garlic *(minced)*

½ Teaspoon of crushed red pepper flakes

1 Cup of smoked Gouda *(cubed)*

DOUGH

1 Cup of all-purpose flour

½ Cup of cake flour

1 Teaspoon of baking powder

½ Tablespoon of garlic powder

½ Tablespoon of chili powder

2 Teaspoons of sugar

8 Ounces of cream cheese *(softened)*

1 Stick of unsalted butter *(softened)*

1 Large egg beaten lightly with 1 teaspoon of water *(Egg wash)*

Directions

Bring three quarts of vegetable or chicken broth to a boil. Add the greens, onions, garlic, and pepper flakes into the pot. Stir well. Cover and reduce the heat to low. Continue to allow the greens to cook for about 45 minutes. Drain the greens and allow them to cool. In the meantime, prepare the dough by placing the dry ingredients into a large bowl. Mix well.

In a separate bowl, use a hand mixer to blend together the cream cheese and butter until well blended. Combine the flour mixture and mix until well incorporated. Place into the refrigerator for an hour.

Sprinkle the counter surface with a light coating of flour. Roll the dough out to about 1/8 inch thick. Use a ring or cutter to cut the dough into 4-inch circles. *(Can be larger if desired)*

Spoon about one tablespoon of greens into the circle. Add 1 cube of cheese on top of the greens. Fold the dough over into a half moon. Use a fork to crimp the edges and seal the dough. Place the empanadas onto a greased cookie sheet. *(Non-stick spray can be used)*

Bake on 400 degrees for 5 minutes. Using a pastry brush, apply the egg wash and continue baking for an additional 10 minutes or until golden brown. Enjoy!

CREAMED PEAS & MUSHROOMS

COOK TIME: 4 MINUTES | **SERVES:** 8

Ingredients

½ Stick of butter

½ Small yellow onion *(chopped)*

4 Baby portabella mushrooms *(sliced)*

2 Cans of green peas

1 Teaspoon of garlic powder

1 Tablespoon of sugar

1 Tablespoon of flour *(all-purpose)*

1 Cup of cream

Salt to taste

Pepper to taste

Directions

Open the peas. Drain the liquid from one of the cans. In a small pot, add the butter, onions, and mushrooms. Sauté the onion and mushrooms for about 2 minutes. Add the peas and continue to cook for about 4 minutes. Add the remaining ingredients and gently stir until smooth. Reduce the heat to low and continue to simmer until creamy. Add more cream if necessary. Serve as a wonderful side dish. Enjoy!

"GOOD OLE" COUNTRY OXTAILS & GRITS

COOK TIME: 2 HOURS | SERVES: 8

Ingredients

OXTAILS

½ Cup of vegetable oil

1 ½ Cups of all-purpose flour

10 Pounds of beef oxtails *(heavy fat trimmed off)*

1 Tablespoon of seasoned salt

½ Tablespoon of black pepper

½ Tablespoon of minced garlic

1 large white onion *(thin sliced)*

½ Cup of Worcestershire sauce

4 Cups of beef broth

GRITS

4 Cups of water

½ Stick of butter *(unsalted)*

1 Teaspoons of salt

12 Tablespoons of stone ground grits

1 Tablespoon of garlic powder

3 Tablespoons of Mascarpone cheese

Directions

Place a large sauce pot onto the stove on medium high. Add the oil to the pot. Coat the oxtails in the flour. Shake off the excess flour and add to the pot. Brown the tails on all sides. Use more oil if necessary. Sprinkle the seasoning over the oxtail. Add the remaining ingredients. Bring the pot to a boil, and cover with a tight lid. Reduce the heat to simmer. Allow the beef to cook for about two hours or until fork tender.

Place a one-quart pot on the stove on high. Pour the water, butter, and salt into the pot. Allow the water to come to a boil. Add the grits to the pot while stirring with a whisk. Cover the grits and reduce to simmer for about 7 minutes. Add the garlic powder and Mascarpone cheese. Stir well and remove from the stove. Spoon the grits into a dinner plate or bowl. Spoon the oxtails and broth over the grits and serve immediately. Enjoy!

NORTH CAROLINA IS AND WILL FOREVER BE THE PORK CAPITAL OF THE SOUTH AND THE UNITED STATES. Pig farms are plentiful in the Tar Heel state, especially in and around the Wilson, Battleboro and Pinetops, areas. I remember as a little boy watching my grandfather slaughter the hogs. It seemed like it would take months to roast a pig, but, in actuality it only took several hours. There's nothing like the taste of a freshly roasted pig. It seemed like every family function or church outing, the chopped BBQ had to be present. It's only right to pay homage to the great farmers of the Carolinas by preparing a wonderful roasted pork belly. This multi-step process will yield a wonderful pork belly that will melt in your mouth and leave you wanting more.

MAPLE & GARLIC ROASTED PORK BELLY

COOK TIME: 2.5 HOURS | SERVES: 10

Ingredients

RUB

¼ Cup of Kosher salt

½ Cup of chopped garlic

1 Teaspoon of dry thyme

½ Tablespoon of fennel seeds

1 Teaspoons of crushed red pepper flakes

½ Cup of brown sugar

½ Cup of olive oil

STOCK

2 Cups of Chardonnay wine

1 Quart of chicken broth

2 Tablespoons of unsalted butter

2 Tablespoons of maple syrup

Directions

Pre-heat oven to 200 degrees. Spray a roasting pan with non-stick. Use a sharp knife to score the skin diagonally from one corner to the other. Turn the pork over the and repeat the same step. Rub the salt, garlic, thyme, fennel, pepper flakes, and sugar over the skin. Make sure to rub well until the seasonings go between the slits of the skin. Place the pan onto the stove over medium high heat. Add the oil to the pan. Once the oil is hot, then place the pork skin side down and Brown the skin for about three minutes. Turn the pork belly over. Add the bay leaves, and wine. Cook until the alcohol burns off which should take about a minute. Next, add the chicken broth and allow the broth to come to a boil. Then place the pan into the oven uncovered and bake for two and a half hours. Remove from the oven and cool.

Slice the pork belly about three inches wide and about 6 inches long. Place a skillet onto the stove and melt the butter. Add the sliced pork belly into the skillet. Spoon the maple syrup onto the pork. Sauté for about two minutes while the coating the belly with the syrup. Add more syrup for additional slices. Enjoy!

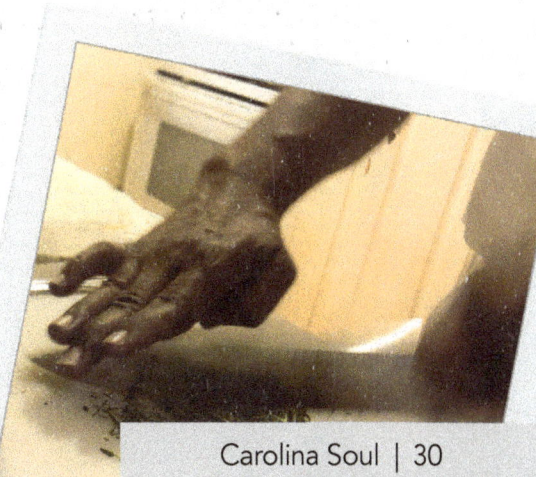

EASTERN CAROLINA BBQ IS ONE OF MY FAVORITE FOODS THAT MY FAMILY ENJOYS WHENEVER WE HAVE AN OPPORTUNITY TO SEE ONE ANOTHER. This is a dish that we often have at Christmas, Thanksgiving or anytime we can see each other. Many methods of preparation have been passed down from generation to generation as to how to properly make BBQ. My cousin Anthony who inherited the recipe and cooking technique from his Uncle Jack Whitaker or Mr. Ogden Batts down in Wallace, NC has one specific method which is excellent. There's nothing like sitting up half the night with the fellas' as we tell funny stories about moments almost too embarrassing to repeat anywhere outside of that circle. My cousin Russell is the pro at taking a story and adding bogus facts. He always says. "I call it as I see it!" as he stuffs his mouth full of chopped BBQ or whatever else he can put his hands on. In the sum total of things that is what it is all about. That's what chopped BBQ does. It brings people together. There's nothing like the smell of the smoke as it fills the air.

NORTH CAROLINA CHOPPED BBQ

COOK TIME: 8-10 MINUTES | SERVINGS VARY

Ingredients

Pork shoulder *(Bone-in)* *(do not trim the fat)*

Pork butt

5 Pounds of lump charcoal

1 Pound of hickory wood pieces

Salt to taste

Pepper to taste

3 Cups of apple cider vinegar

1 Cup of water

½ Cup of brown sugar

1 Tablespoon of crushed red pepper flakes

¾ Cup of ketchup

Directions

Wash the pork shoulder and pork butt with cold water. Then, place the pork shoulder and pork butt in a roasting pan. Pat dry with a paper towel. In the meantime, Place the lump charcoal and hickory wood chips into the grill or smoker and light with a blow torch or lighter fluid. While the coals are getting hot, season the shoulder and butt with the salt and pepper. Rub the salt and pepper over the meat as evenly as possible. The grill or smoker should be around 250 degrees by this time. Next, place the shoulder and butt onto the grill or smoker. Place the fat "side down" and cook. Close the grill and allow the meat to cook for about 8-10 hours.

Next is the sauce, place a small pot onto the stove. Add the vinegar, water, brown sugar, crushed red peppers, ketchup into the pot. Mix well. Allow the sauce to come to a simmer. Turn off the heat. Cover and set aside for later use.

Once the pork is done. Remove from the grill or smoker and place into a roasting pan. Cover with foil until cooled. Once the pork is cooled, began to pull the pork. Combine the shoulder and butt together and chop with a cleaver. Once the pork is completely chopped, pour the sauce over the pork. Mix well. Serve on a bun with coleslaw or with a side of hushpuppies. Enjoy!

BLACKEYE PEA & SAUSAGE SOUP

COOK TIME: 20 MINUTES | **SERVES:** 6 - 8

Ingredients

1 Tablespoon of olive oil

1 Tablespoon of unsalted butter

1 Yellow onion *(chopped)*

1 Small green bell pepper *(chopped)*

2 Tablespoons of fresh garlic *(fine chopped)*

1 ½ Pounds of ground sweet Italian sausage

2 Bay leaves

1 Pound of black-eye peas *(rinsed and picked through for foreign objects)*

3 Quarts of chicken stock

1 Teaspoon of season salt

1 Teaspoon of crushed red pepper

½ Cup of white wine

2 Cups of chopped kale

Directions

Place a 5-quart pot onto the stove over medium high heat. Add the olive oil and butter inside the pot. Once the butter is melted, add the onion, bell pepper, and garlic. Sautee for about four minutes. Add the sausage and bay leaves. Cook until the sausage is browned. Add the peas, chicken stock, salt, and pepper flakes. Bring to a boil. Once the soup is boiling, cover and reduce the heat to low. Cook for about three hours. Add the wine and kale. Continue to cook for another 20 minutes. Spoon into a bowl. Serve with a slice of my sweet potato corn bread. Enjoy!

MUSSELS & COUSCOUS SALAD

COOK TIME: 4 MINUTES | SERVES: 8

Ingredients

2 Sticks of butter *(unsalted)*

1 White onion *(chopped)*

1 Teaspoon of crushed red pepper flakes

1 Cup of white wine

4 Cups of chicken broth

1 Tablespoon of minced garlic

Pinch of salt

1 Red bell pepper *(diced)*

1 ½ Cups of chopped kale

2 Pounds of fresh mussels

3 Cups of couscous

Juice of ½ lemon

¼ Cup of extra virgin olive oil

1 Tablespoon of flat leaf parsley *(chopped)*

Directions

In a 5-quart pot, add the butter, onions, pepper flakes, wine, broth, garlic, salt, bell pepper, and kale. Allow the stock to come to a simmer. Add the mussels and cover. Cook until the mussels are open. Spoon the broth over the mussels. Cook for about 4 minutes. Drain the broth from the mussels. Pour the hot broth evenly over the couscous. Mix well and cover. Place the couscous into the refrigerator to chill. Arrange the couscous into a bowl or serving platter. Place the mussels throughout the couscous. Drizzle the lemon juice, 1 cup of the broth from the mussels and olive oil over the salad. Garnish with the chopped parsley. Enjoy!

ROME'S COLESLAW

PREP TIME: 5 MINUTES | SERVES: 10

Ingredients

1 Head of Napa cabbage *(washed and shredded)*

½ Head of purple cabbage

2 Large carrots *(finely shredded)*

1 Small pineapple *(thinly sliced)*

4 Mangos *(thinly sliced)*

¼ Cup of sliced almonds

½ Cup of mint leaves *(whole)*

½ Large Vidalia onion *(thin sliced)*

½ Cup of apple juice

¼ Cup of Dijon mustard

¼ Cup of real mayonnaise

4 Tablespoons of sugar

4 Tablespoons of apple cider vinegar

1 Teaspoon of cayenne pepper

Salt and pepper to taste

Directions

In a large mixing bowl, combine the cabbage(s), carrot, pineapple, mango, almonds, mint leaves and onion. Toss well. In a smaller bowl, combine the remaining ingredients. Mix well. Add the sauce to the cabbage and fruit mixture. Toss well, cover and refrigerate until ready for use. Enjoy!

MY AUNT BETTE HAS ALWAYS BEEN VERY SPECIAL TO ME. No matter what, I can depend on her to always show up with a great dish. However, Aunt Bette, like a lot of our older relatives never measure any ingredients. It's amazing how delicious things consistently seem to turn. I asked her for the recipe and how long she cooked the neck bones but she never answered me. The next time I saw her she took me aside and whispered quietly. *"Cook them until they get done."*

I asked her for the recipe and how long she cooked the neck bones but *she never answered me.* **The next time I saw her she took me aside and whispered quietly. "COOK THEM UNTIL THEY GET DONE."**

AUNT BETTE'S
BBQ NECK BONES

COOK TIME: 1 HOUR AND 30 MINUTES | SERVES: 8

Ingredients

3 Pounds of pork neck bones *(beef neck bones can be used as a substitute)*

½ Cup of cider vinegar

1 ½ Cup of water

1 ½ Teaspoons of crushed red pepper flakes

2 Cups of ketchup

1 Tablespoons of liquid smoke

½ Cup of maple syrup

¼ Cup of brown sugar

¼ Cup of Worcestershire sauce

1 ½ Teaspoons of salt

1 Teaspoon of black pepper

Directions

PREHEAT THE OVEN TO 375 DEGREES. Place the neck bones in a large pot and cover with cold water. Bring the pot to a boil. Boil for 15 minutes. Drain the water out of the pot repeating the step. Once the pot is drained for the second time, remove the neck bones from the pot and place them inside a roaster. Pour the vinegar and water over the neck bones. Cover with foil and place in the oven. Bake for two hours. In the meantime, place a small pot onto the stove. Combine all the remaining ingredients into the pot. Mix well. Allow the pot to come to a simmer and continue to stir until the sauce is well blended. Remove the roaster from the oven and ladle the sauce over the neck bones.

REDUCE THE OVEN TO 325. Place the neck bones back into the oven uncovered and continue to cook for an additional 30 minutes. Enjoy!

MY FATHER WAS AN EXCELLENT COOK. When he was in the army he was the mess steward or mess sergeant as we use to call them. In other words, he oversaw the dining facility. He kept a lot of the old recipes that was used back in his day. Some of the old favorites became masterpieces at the family "get togethers." I will never forget the day that I walked into his kitchen and he said to me, "I'm sure you don't know anything about this recipe so pay attention." He'd always say that I was too young to get the full recipe and that I should wait until I was of a ripe old age to receive the family secret recipes.

I will never forget the day that I walked into his kitchen and he said to me, **"I'M SURE YOU DON'T KNOW ANYTHING ABOUT THIS RECIPE SO PAY ATTENTION."**

BRAISED BEEF SHORT RIBS

COOK TIME: **3** HOURS | SERVES: **4 - 6**

Ingredients

4 Pounds of short ribs *(bone in or out)*

½ Cup of all-purpose flour

2 Teaspoons of coarse black pepper

2 Teaspoons of salt

½ Cup of olive oil

1 Teaspoon of dry thyme

1 Tablespoon of minced garlic

1 Yellow onion *(sliced)*

2 Cups of beef broth

½ Cup of Worcestershire sauce

½ Cup of merlot

White or yellow rice for serving *(follow directions on the package)*

Directions

PREHEAT THE OVEN TO 350 DEGREES. In a medium stainless-steel bowl, combine the flour, pepper, and salt. Mix well. Place the skillet on the stove on medium high heat. Once the skillet is hot, add the oil to the skillet. Coat the ribs in the flour. Shake off the extra flour and place the ribs into the oil. Brown the ribs on all side. Place the ribs into a large roaster. Add the thyme, garlic, onion, broth, Worcestershire sauce, and wine. Cover with a tight-fitting lid or foil. Bake for 3 hours. Serve over rice. Enjoy!

ROME'S SWEET POTATO CORN BREAD

COOK TIME: 25 MINUTES | SERVES: 24

Ingredients

2 Large sweet potatoes *(peeled and sliced into 1 inch)*

½ Cup of sugar

½ Cup of brown sugar

1 Stick of unsalted butter

2 Teaspoons of ground nutmeg

1 Tablespoon of vanilla extract

¼ Cup of orange juice *(with or without pulp)*

2 Cup of yellow corn meal

2 Cup of cake flour

8 Teaspoons of baking powder

½ Teaspoon of salt

3 Eggs

¾ Cup of milk

4 Tablespoons of oil

½ Cup of honey

1 Stick of melted butter

Directions

PREHEAT THE OVEN TO 400 DEGREES.

Place a 5-quart sauce pot on the stove over medium high. Place the potatoes into the pot. Add the sugars, butter, nutmeg, extract, and orange juice. Cover with a tight-fitting lid. Cook until the potatoes are fork tender. About 25 minutes. Remove the lid and whip the potatoes until smooth. Set aside. Do not cover.

In a medium to large bowl, combine the corn meal, flour, baking powder, salt, eggs, milk, and oil. Mix well but do not overmix. Add the sweet potatoes to the mix and blend well.

Spray the oven pans with non-stick spray or use muffin liners. Fill each cup with the batter about three quarters full. Place the muffins into the oven and back for about 20-25 minutes. Test the muffins with a toothpick. Brush the muffins with honey and melted butter. Enjoy!

43 | Carolina Soul

UNCLE LARRY WAS THE YOUNGEST OF MY MOTHER'S SIBLINGS. Every fish fry or cookout or Sunday meal, we could expect to see Uncle Larry cooking something. But the thing that we looked forward to the most was his hushpuppies. It always seemed like it took him forever to finish cooking them. But it was probably due to the fact that we were stealing them as he was cooking them. As soon as he would turn his head or walk away for a moment, it would be an all-out assault on the hushpuppies. If he caught you, he would curse you out and tell you "Don't bring your ass back over here until the food is ready!" Rest in Peace Uncle Larry. His famous sweet hushpuppies lives on.

As soon as he would turn his head or walk away for a moment, it would be an **ALL-OUT ASSAULT ON THE HUSHPUPPIES.**

UNCLE LARRY'S
SWEET HUSHPUPPIES

COOK TIME: 5 | SERVINGS WILL VARY

Ingredients

3 Cups of yellow cornmeal

2 Teaspoons of baking powder

¾ Cup of self-rising flour

½ Cup of sugar

Pinch of salt

1 ½ Cups of milk

½ Cup of water

1 Egg beaten

1 Small yellow onion *(minced)*

½ Gallon of vegetable oil

Directions

In a large bowl, combine all the dry ingredients. Add the milk, water, egg, and onion. Mix well, cover and set aside for about 15 minutes.

In a large pot or cast-iron skillet, heat the oil until it reaches a temperature of 360 degrees. Once the oil is hot, use a tablespoon or small ice cream scoop to place the batter into the oil. Fry the hushpuppies until golden brown all over. Cook the hushpuppies for about 5 minutes. Place them on a paper towel to drain. I feel it's my duty to warn you. My experience has taught me that those around you won't want to wait. With, keep a close eye on the hushpuppies. Enjoy!

TATER JACK TURNOVERS

COOK TIME: 15 - 20 MINUTES | SERVES: 12

Ingredients

SWEET POTATOES

4 Large sweet potatoes *(peeled and sliced about an inch and a half thick)*

1 ¼ Cup of sugar

½ Cup of brown sugar

2 Teaspoons of grated orange peel

1 Teaspoon of fresh ground nutmeg

1 Teaspoon of ground cinnamon

1 Teaspoon of ground mace

½ Cup of Carnation milk

DOUGH

2 ½ Cups of all-purpose flour

1 Teaspoon of baking powder

½ Teaspoon of salt

¾ Cup of shortening

8 Tablespoons of ice cold water

1 Egg (beaten)

½ Cup of milk

1 Tablespoon each of cinnamon and white sugar *(mix together and reserve for later use)*

Directions

PREHEAT THE OVEN TO 400 DEGREES. Place the sweet potatoes in a large pot and boil until fork tender. Drain the potatoes and place them into a large mixing bowl. Whip the potatoes until smooth. Add the sugars and spices. Combine the milk with the mixture and mix until well blended. Set aside until ready for use.

For the dough, combine the flour, baking soda and salt in a bowl. Add the shortening and mix until well blended but resembling coarse cornmeal. Gradually add the water and mix until the dough forms a ball. Don't overmix the dough. In a small bowl, combine the egg and milk. Mix well and set aside until ready for use.

Divide the dough into 12 portions. Add a sprinkle of flour over the service of your table or counter. Roll each portion into a 6-inch circle. Spoon ¼ to 1/3 cup of filling on half of each circle. Moisten edges with the egg and milk mixture. Seal the edges with a fork.

Place on a greased baking sheets. Brush with the milk and egg mixture. Sprinkle with cinnamon and sugar mixture. Cut slits in the top. Bake for 15-20 minutes or until golden brown. Enjoy!

THERE'S TWO THINGS THAT I ENJOY THAT ARE NAMESAKES OF NORTH CAROLINA; PEPSI *(IT'S KNOWN AS "THE TASTE OF THE CAROLINAS")* **AND MUSCADINE GRAPES BETTER KNOWN AS SCUPPERNONG.** It's our nation's first cultivated grape. From New Bern North Carolina, which is the birth place of Pepsi, to the shores of North Carolina, these two ingredients have combined in this book to create a wonderful pork chop to rival all others. I'm a huge pork chop fan and you will be as well after this dish.

There's two things that I enjoy that are namesakes of **NORTH CAROLINA;** **PEPSI** *(It's known as "the taste of the Carolinas")* AND **MUSCADINE GRAPES** *BETTER KNOWN AS SCUPPERNONG.*

GRILLED PORK CHOPS
BATHED IN
PEPSI MUSCADINE REDUCTION

COOK TIME: 5 MINUTES | SERVES: 8

Ingredients

8 Thick cut pork chops *(washed and patted dry)*

1 Cup of all-purpose flour

2 Teaspoons of salt

1 Teaspoon of coarse black pepper

1 Teaspoon of garlic powder

1 ½ Cup of vegetable oil

1 Stick of butter *(unsalted)*

½ Cup of sugar

2 Cups of Muscadine grapes *(hulls and seeds removed)*

2 Cup of water

1 Can of Pepsi

Directions

Place a large skillet on the stove over medium high. In a large bowl or plastic bag, combine the flour, salt, pepper, and garlic powder. Mix well. Add the oil to the skillet and allow to heat for about 5 minutes. Once the oil is hot, coat the chops with the flour mixture. Shake off any excess flour and place them into the oil. Cook the chops on both sides for about five minutes. Once the chops are cooked, drain well on a paper towel. Remove the oil from the skillet. Place the butter in the skillet along with the sugar and grapes. Mix well and bring to a simmer. Cook for about twenty minutes. Add the water and continue to cook until the liquid reduces to half the amount. Add the chops to the sauce. Pour the soda over the chops and cover. Cook for about twenty minutes on low or until the chops are tender. Serve over rice. Enjoy!

EVERY ONCE IN A WHILE, MY DAUGHTER AND I WILL TAKE A LONG ROAD TRIP ACROSS DIFFERENT AREAS OF THE TARHEEL STATE. There's something about pulling up to a gas station just off a country road for refreshment. Jasmine and I have this thing about boiled peanuts.

BOILED PEANUTS

COOK TIME: 30 | SERVINGS WILL VARY

Ingredients

4 Pounds of peanuts

5 Tablespoons of salt

1 Package of dry crab boil

2 Tablespoons of garlic powder

1 Tablespoon of crushed red pepper flakes

3 Tablespoons of Cajon seasoning

4 Gallons of water

Directions

Wash the peanuts in cold water. Drain and repeat the step. Soak the peanuts in cold water for about 30 minutes. Drain and rinse once again. Add the seasoning and peanuts to the crockpot and cover with cold water. Cover and cook for up to four hours. Enjoy!

BLACKEYE PEAS & OKRA

COOK TIME: 30 MINUTES | SERVES: 4 - 6

Ingredients

½ Stick of salted butter

1 Small onion *(chopped)*

2 Strips of bacon

2 Pounds of frozen black eye-peas

1 Bay leaf

½ Teaspoon of crushed red pepper flakes

1 Teaspoon of black pepper

1 Teaspoon of sugar

1 Teaspoon of salt

1 tablespoon of chopped garlic or garlic powder

5 Cups of chicken broth

½ Pound of frozen okra *(whole or cut)*

Directions

Place a two-quart pot on the stove on medium high. Add the butter, onion, and bacon. Allow the bacon to cook until crispy. Add the seasonings and chicken broth. Stir well. Bring to a boil. Cover with a lid and reduce the heat to simmer. Cook for about 30 minutes. Add the okra and cook for an additional 4 minutes. Enjoy!

BOUDIN STUFFED QUAIL

COOK TIME: 10 MINUTES | SERVES: 4 - 6

Ingredients

1 Cup of jerk marinade

2 Whole quails *(split in half)*

½ Pound of pork roast

¼ Pound of pork liver

1 Cup of long grain rice

1 Small yellow onion *(chopped)*

3 Cloves of crushed garlic *(chopped)*

1 Tablespoon of Cajon seasoning

1 Teaspoon of cayenne seasoning

½ Cup of diced green onion tops

Kosher salt to taste

Cracked black pepper to taste

Dash of pepper sauce

Directions

PREHEAT THE OVEN TO 400 DEGREES. Place the halved quails into a gallon size zip lock bag. Pour the marinade into the bag. Seal the bag and place into the refrigerator for at least an hour. In the meantime, in a heavy pot with a tight-fitting lid, add the pork roast and fill the pot with water to a depth of 4 inches over the pork. Cover, place in the oven and cook for 2 hours or until falling apart. Remove the pork from the pot reserving the cooking liquid.

Add the liver to the pot with just enough cooking liquid to cover. Bring the pot to a boil for about 10 minutes. Remove the liver from the pot and drain well. Do not discard the liquid. Cook the rice according to the directions on the box using the liquid from the pork.

In a food processor, pulse the meat and liver along with the yellow onion and garlic until it reaches a smooth, yet chunky consistency. Do not over mix to a mushy stage.

Add the rice in a ratio of 80% meat to 20% rice. Gradually add some of the cooking liquid from the liver until the mixture is moist. Add the remaining ingredients and mix gently until all the ingredients are evenly incorporated.

Take the quail out of the refrigerator and drain well. Place them into a casserole baking dish. Use your index finger to gently lift the skin partially from the breast of the quail. Use a teaspoon to carefully spoon the stuffing under the skin. Place the quail into the oven and bake for about 10 minutes. Remove the quail from the oven. Place over a bed of yellow rice if desired. Enjoy!

Carolina Corn Pudding

As a chef, I can tell you that I've cooked corn or seen it cooked hundreds of ways, *but nothing beats the taste of* **FRESH CORN RIGHT OUT OF THE FIELD.**

MY AUNT BESSIE LOVES HERSELF SOME CORN PUDDING. I guess growing up on a farm can do that to you. Back in the day when we were in North Carolina visiting for the holidays, I can remember jumping in the car and riding into town with my grandfather and clearly seeing the country roads being lined with corn fields on both sides seemingly for miles. I could smell the sweetness of the fresh corn and in my mind, I could taste the butter as it would drip down my arms. I miss those days. As a chef, I can tell you that I've cooked corn or seen it cooked hundreds of ways, but nothing beats the taste of fresh corn right out of the field. This is a simple recipe, however; execution is key to your success. The taste will amaze you!

AUNT BESSIE'S
CAROLINA CORN PUDDING

COOK TIME: 30 MINUTES | SERVES: 8

Ingredients

2 Strips of country bacon *(chopped)*

1 Small shallot (chopped)

1 Ears of fresh corn *(off the cob)*

1 Can of cream corn

2 Teaspoons of sugar

8 Ounces of sour cream

1 Box of Jiffy cornbread

1 Stick of salted butter

Directions

PREHEAT THE OVEN TO 350 DEGREES. Place a large skillet on the stove on medium high heat. Next, add the chopped bacon and shallot. Sautee for about two minutes and then add the fresh corn. Continue cooking for an additional five minutes or until the corn is cooked through. Pour the mixture into a bowl and add the cream corn, sugar, sour cream, and cornbread. Mix well and set aside.

Place the butter into a 2-quart casserole dish. Place the dish into the oven and melt the butter. Remove the dish from the oven and add the corn mixture. Return the dish to the oven and bake for 30 minutes. The top should be golden brown. Spoon unto the place. This is the perfect side dish to accompany your Sunday meal or your holiday feast. Enjoy!

I LOVE TALKING ABOUT MY FRIENDS AND THEIR EATING HABITS. Especially those who really appreciate great food. Chris Wilcox and his beautiful wife Tiffany loves fresh seafood. He is from Whiteville, North Carolina and has accessibility to the Carolina coast seafood most of the year. Carolina blue crab is meaty and naturally sweet. When combined with this pasta dish, the taste buds will crave for more every time. *Just Ask Chris!*

CAROLINA BLUE CRAB is meaty and naturally sweet.

WEEZY'S
LUMP CRAB AND PASTA

COOK TIME: 20 MINUTES | SERVES: 10

Ingredients

2 Pounds of linguini noodles *(cooked)*

½ Tablespoon of salt

2 Tablespoons of olive oil

4 Cloves of crushed garlic

2 Tablespoons of oyster sauce

½ Cup of parmesan cheese

3 Tablespoons of garlic powder

½ Stick of unsalted butter

Course black pepper to taste

2 Teaspoons of chicken base

1 ½ Pounds of fresh lump crab *(picked, shells removed)*

Directions

Bring two gallons of water to a boil. Add the salt to the water. Stir in the pasta to prevent sticking. Cook the pasta for about 9 minutes or until al dente. Pour the pasta into a strainer and rinse with cold water to stop the cooking process.

Place a large skillet onto the stove and heat on medium high. Add the olive oil, garlic and oyster sauce and stir until well blended. Do not burn the garlic. Reduce the heat to medium low. Add the pasta and bring back up to temperature. Add the remaining ingredients and toss well. Serve immediately. Enjoy!

MY FRIEND TIFFANY WILCOX IS A HUGE FAN OF THIS RECIPE. She is a young lady who always tries to keep her girlish figure in tact until this dish is prepared. At that point, I think all bets are off.

I love going to the market and getting great cuts of thin pork chops for this dish. The cooking time plays a role in why I choose to use the thin cut as opposed to the thicker chop. Of course, if you have a little extra time on your hands to let the chops cook longer, by all means go for it. If you don't have time to slave all day in the kitchen, the thin chop of the center cut will serve you well for this recipe

If you don't have time to slave all day in the kitchen, **THE THIN CHOP OF THE CENTER CUT** *will serve you well for this recipe.*

BROWN SUGAR GLAZED PORK CHOPS

COOK TIME: 15 MINUTES | SERVES: 4

Ingredients

4 Center cut pork chops

½ Cup of all-purpose flour

Salt and black Pepper to taste

1 Teaspoon of garlic powder

1 Teaspoon of ground ginger

1 Cup of vegetable oil

1 Cup of diced pineapple

¾ Cup of pineapple juice

¼ Cup of brown sugar

¼ Cup of spice rum *(I like the captain)*

Directions

Rinse the chops off under cold water. Pat dry with a paper towel and set aside on a platter. In the meantime, combine the flour, salt, pepper, garlic powder, and ginger. Mix well.

Place a large skillet on the stove and preheat on medium high. Add the oil. Coat the chops in the flour mixture. Shake off the extra flour and carefully place into the skillet. Sautee the chops for about 3 minutes on each side.

Remove the chops from the skillet and place on a platter to drain on paper towels. In the meantime, add the pineapple, juice and brown sugar. Stir until the brown sugar is free of any lumps. Add the rum and mix well. Return the chops to the skillet. Ladle the sauce over the chops. Cover with a tight-fitting lid and reduce the heat to medium low. Continue to cook for about 15 minutes. The sauce should coat the chops well. I recommend this dish over rice. Enjoy!

THERE WAS A MAN BY THE NAME OF JOE RICH. HE WAS ORIGINALLY FROM PENSACOLA, FLORIDA. During my sixth-grade year of high school, I moved to Ohio to live with him and his wife. Often, he would reflect on his days as a soldier in the US Navy. I can remember him reflecting on his time spent on kitchen patrol with the cooks. He told me about a good old mess steward (military Chef) who could really cook. Apparently, something happened where the mess steward couldn't get a shipment in on time as they were out to sea and due to the severe weather there was no way to get the supplies needed for food. Mr. Rich said he listened to the mess steward complain for about an hour as he tried to figure out how he was going to pull off the next meal. Joe suggested to him to make some beans and franks. The mess steward looked at him and said, "I'm not making no damn beans and franks. Who the hell eats beans and franks?" Low and behold, he had no other choice. He took Joe's recipe and advice. The soldiers began to request beans and franks as a weekly meal. Sometimes the simple things mean so much. Since that time, I've created my own rendition of this childhood comfort dish.

> The soldiers began to request beans and franks as a weekly meal. **Sometimes the simple things MEAN SO MUCH.**

OLD SCHOOL
BEANIES AND WEENIES

COOK TIME: 1 HOUR | SERVES: 10

Ingredients

1 Large can of plain pork and beans

4 Strips of bacon

1 Medium onion *(chopped)*

1 Green bell pepper *(chopped)*

1 Pound of hot ground Italian sausage

1 Pound of hot dogs (sliced)

1 Cup of brown sugar

1 Cup of white sugar

1 Tablespoon of cinnamon

2 Tablespoons of vanilla extract

¼ Cup of yellow mustard

1 ½ Cups of frosted flakes *(crushed)*

Directions

Pour the beans into your favorite roaster or casserole dish and set aside for later use. Place a large skillet on the stove over medium high. Once the skillet is heated up (about 5 minutes) 'add the bacon, onion, and bell pepper to the skillet and cook until the bacon is done. Pour the mixture into the beans and mix until well blended. Add the sausage to the skillet and cook it until it's done. Add the sausage and franks to the beans along with the sugars, cinnamon, vanilla, and mustard. Give the beans a good stir and then place into the oven. Bake for an hour. Remove the beans and franks from the oven. Spread the frosted flakes over the beans and return to the oven and continue cooking for an additional thirty minutes. Remove and enjoy!

MY MOTHER COULD REALLY COOK, LIKE SO MANY MOTHERS ALL OVER THE WORLD SHE COULD CREATE SOMETHING OUT OF NOTHING. That's what I love about people in the south. It doesn't take much to create a meal out of nothing. Especially when you're financially challenged at times. Holidays were no different. We didn't always know where the food came from or where momma was going to have enough to create the master piece of a meal we were expecting but somehow, she always made it happen. My mother had a habit of inviting people we didn't even know to dinner. I never knew why. Some of those people just came from off the street as far as I knew. I would be pissed. I can recall thinking, who is this person and why the hell is your plate bigger than mine? I mean seriously! I knew ministry starts at home, but who were these new family members we never heard of? LOL!

Either way, one of the simplest meals that she would prepare would be her neck bones and rice. Those meaty neck bones would cook down until they were tender. They were always seasoned to perfection. Once she got the broth just like she wanted it, and the necks were as tender as they should be, she would add in the rice. I promise you, the leftover rice, if there was any, would make the perfect meal by itself. This was a true delicacy in our household. Sometimes she would switch it up to turkey necks and rice. My friend Bren loves this dish.

NECK BONES & RICE

COOK TIME: 1 HOUR | SERVES: 10

Ingredients

10 Meaty neck bones

1 Gallon of chicken or turkey broth

Pinch of crushed red pepper flakes

1 Large onion *(diced)*

1 Tablespoon of black pepper

2 Tablespoons of salt

3 Cups of white rice

Directions

In a two-and-a-half-gallon pot, add the neck bones and enough water to cover. Bring the neck bones to a boil. Once the neck bones boil for about five minutes, discard the water. Refill the pot with the chicken broth. Add the onions, peppers, and salt. Bring to a boil. Cover with a tight-fitting lid and reduce the heat to medium low or simmer. Cook for about an hour. Once the neck bones are fork tender, stir in the rice and continue cooking until the rice is done. This dish will as they say, make you slap somebody. Enjoy!

I ABSOLUTELY LOVE MEATLOAF. There's nothing like it. It's just a good old American tradition. My mother would usually top it with a little spiked ketchup. But through the years I've tried a few diverse ways of recreating this American tradition. Even when I switch it up and use turkey instead of ground beef, it comes out amazing.

My young cousin Dakari is a meatloaf fanatic. I've created a southwestern style, Italian, Greek, Caribbean, BBQ, and even Asian version of a meatloaf. You name it, I've done it all. But the one I love the most is my Marsala Meatloaf. If you've ever enjoyed a chicken marsala, you can just about figure how this is going to taste. This recipe has made a wonderful sandwich over the years.

MARSALA MEATLOAF

COOK TIME: 55 MINUTES | SERVES: 8

Ingredients

2 Pounds of ground beef or ground turkey

½ Cup of Worcestershire sauce

1 Package of Lipton soup mix

½ Cup of steak sauce

½ Tablespoon of ground thyme

½ Tablespoon of garlic powder

1 Tablespoon of seasoned salt

2 Eggs *(slightly beaten)*

1 Tablespoon of olive oil

½ Stick of unsalted butter

1 Small onion (thin sliced)

1 Small green bell pepper *(thin sliced)*

1 Cup of mushrooms
(use a variety if desired)

½ Cup of all-purpose flour

¼ Cup of dry sherry and ½ Cup of beef broth

Directions

PREHEAT THE OVEN TO 375 DEGREES. Place a large mixing bowl onto the counter. Add the meat, Worcestershire sauce, soup mix, steak sauce, thyme, garlic powder, season salt, eggs, and olive oil. Mix well. Transfer the mixture onto a greased cookie sheet. Mold into the desired shape. Cover with foil and place into the oven. Cook for about 40 minutes.

Place a large skillet onto the stove on medium high. Add the butter, onion, bell pepper, and mushrooms. Sauté for about three minutes. Add the flour and stir with a whisk until smooth. While stirring, add the sherry and broth. Continue to stir until smooth and no lumps remain. Reduce and simmer until thickened. Remove the meatloaf from the oven and spoon over the meatloaf. Return to the oven and continue cooking for about 12-15 minutes. Remove the meatloaf from the oven and place it onto the stove. Allow it to cool for about 15 minutes before slicing. Serve over mashed potatoes or rice. Enjoy!

I LOVE CAT FISH. I laugh at my sister Tricia. She won't eat it. She says she can't get past the fact that they have whiskers like a real cat. But I say, "That's more for me." Stewed fish is a delicacy in many countries. However, it is my opinion, the Carolinas do it best. I'm sure the good folks of Mississippi and New Orleans may have something to say about that. Bullhead catfish is indigenous to the Carolinas. If you ever hook one, the fight is amazing and a lot of fun to say the least. They are among the smaller type of catfish species and very tasty when fried or prepared any way you like catfish.

BULLHEAD CATFISH STEW

COOK TIME: **20** MINUTES | SERVES: **4**

Ingredients

¼ Cup of vegetable oil

½ Stick of salted butter

1 Onion *(chopped)*

1 Red bell pepper *(chopped)*

1 Fennel bulb *(chopped)*

1 Teaspoon of fresh thyme

1 Can of tomato sauce

½ Tablespoon of sugar

2 Cups of chicken broth

1 Tablespoon of tomato paste

2 Tablespoons of fresh chopped parsley

2 ½ Pounds of fresh catfish nuggets or fillets

Directions

Place a two and a half-gallon pot onto the stove on medium high. Add the oil and butter. Allow the oil to heat up but not burn the butter. Add the onions, bell pepper, fennel, and thyme. Sautee' for about four minutes. Add the tomato sauce, sugar, and chicken broth and stir until well blended. Cover with a lid and simmer for about twenty minutes. Stir in the tomato paste, pepper sauce, and parsley. Mix well and continue to cook for an additional ten minutes. Add the catfish. Cover the pan with a lid and cook for fifteen minutes on medium low. Enjoy!

CAPE FEAR IS ONE OF MY FAVORITE AREAS OFF THE COAST OF NORTH CAROLINA. I was introduced to Bald Head Island four or five years ago. The Atlantic Ocean and Wilmington beach are filled with wonderful attractions and must-see spots. I can't begin to name every restaurant in the area. However, if you're ever there, some of my favorite spots are Dock Street Oyster Bar, Pin Point Restaurant, The Dixie Grill, and Circa 1922 just to name a few. There's something for everyone regardless of your taste buds! I would have to say that Cape Fear Boil Company is my favorite spot. It's located at Carolina Beach, you owe it to yourself to go for a visit. You won't be disappointed.

CAROLINA SHRIMP BOIL

COOK TIME: 20 MINUTES | SERVES: 10

Ingredients

1 ½ Pound of butter

2 Teaspoons of crushed red pepper

4 Bay leaves

2 40-ounce bottles of beer

3 Bags of shrimp boil seasoning

1 Cup of Old bay seasoning

½ Cup of Cajon seasoning

3 Oranges (halved)

4 Lemons (halved)

5 Pounds of small red potatoes

5 Pounds of cut smoked sausage

15 Ears of corn (broke in half)

12 Cloves of crushed garlic

10 Pounds of jumbo shrimp *(deveined, peel on) (head on is optional but encouraged)*

Directions

Place a large 5-gallon pot on a burner. Add in all the ingredients except for the shrimp. Bring to a boil, cover and continue to cook for about 20 minutes. Add the shrimp and continue to cook for an additional 10 minutes. Enjoy!

Carolina Soul | 68

THERE'S AN ONGOING DEBATE ABOUT WHAT SHOULD *GO* ON OR *INTO* GRITS. There's a significant difference between those who live up north and those who live down south. My friend Brevin Knight always sprinkles sugar on his grits. I say he needs to stick with cream of wheat if that's what he wants to do. I personally must have my cheddar or parmesan cheese in my grits. Then there is the debate over how to make them as creamy as possible. Do I add the salt and butter first or do I soak my grits at all? Well, it's simple, it's your choice. The one thing I will tell you is this, *I HATE INSTANT GRITS!!!!!* That's right up there with INSTANT RICE. It should be a sin. For my grits lovers out there, I invite you to enjoy this wonderful dish. I even added my secret ingredient.

My friend *Brevin Knight* always sprinkles sugar on his grits. **I say he needs to stick with cream of wheat** if that's what he wants to do.

GARLIC & CHEDDAR SHRIMP AND GRITS

COOK TIME: 35 MINUTES | SERVES: 4

Ingredients

4 Cups of water

2 Teaspoons of salt

1 Tablespoon of garlic powder

3 Tablespoons of unsalted butter

1 Cup of stone ground grits

1 Tablespoon of Mascarpone cheese

½ Cup of cheddar cheese

1 Tablespoon of olive oil

1 Tablespoon of salted butter

1 Teaspoon of old bay seasoning

1 Teaspoon of garlic powder

1 Tablespoon of pepper sauce

¼ Cup of chicken broth

2 ½ Pounds of large shrimp
(peeled & deveined)

Directions

Place a heavy bottom sauce pot onto the stove. Add the water, salt, garlic and butter. Bring to a boil. Pour in the grits while stirring with a whisk at the same time. This will prevent lumps.

Cover and reduce the heat to simmer. Stir occasionally to prevent sticking. Cook for about 35 minutes. Stir in the Mascarpone and cheddar cheeses. Stir well and set aside.

Place a large skillet on the stove over medium high. Add the olive oil, butter, old bay seasoning, garlic, pepper sauce, and chicken broth. Bring to a simmer. Add the shrimp and continue to cook for about 7 minutes or until the shrimp is pink. To serve, spoon the grits into a bowl or plate. Spoon the shrimp and sauce over the grits. Enjoy!

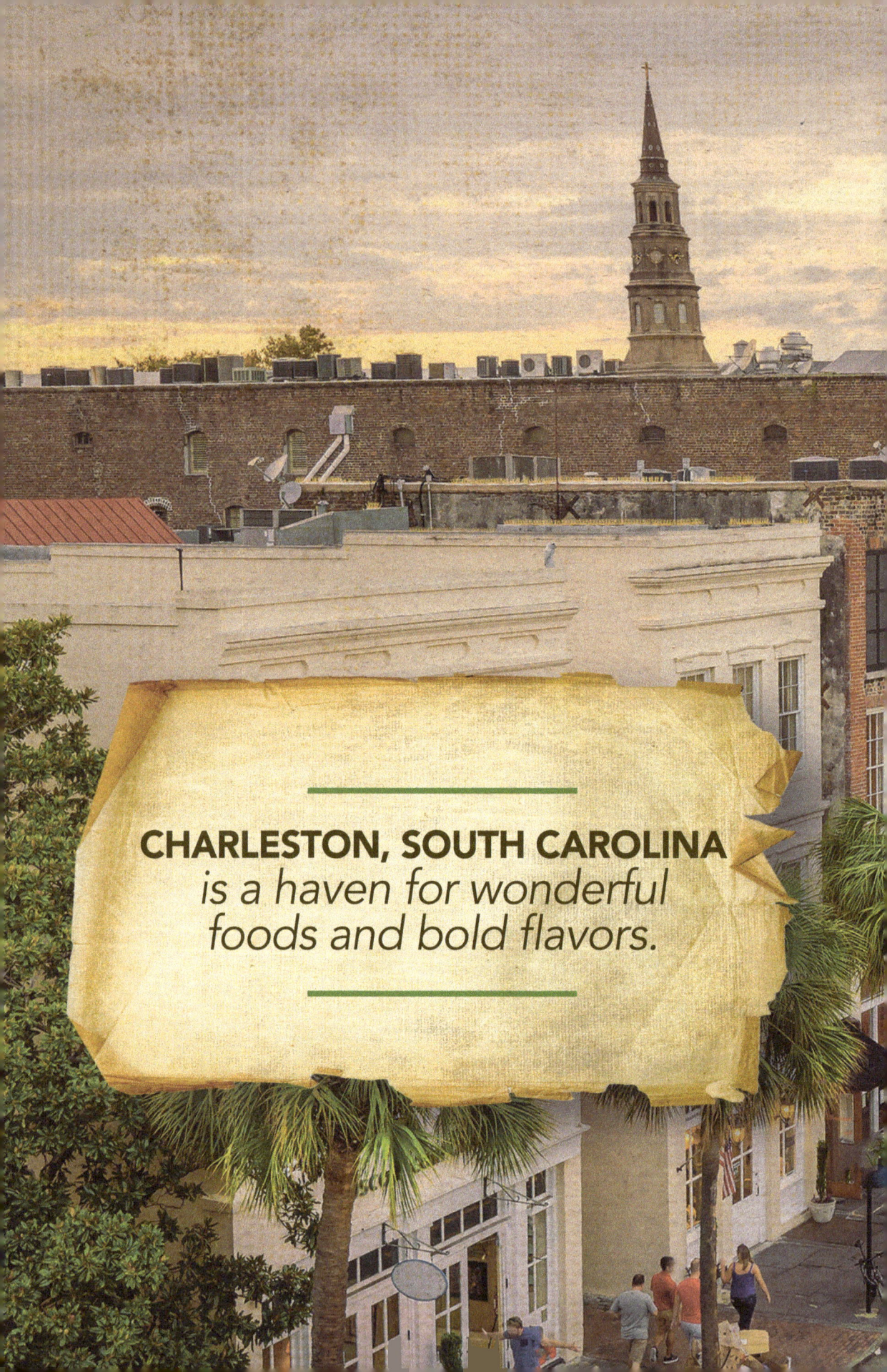

CHARLESTON, SOUTH CAROLINA
is a haven for wonderful foods and bold flavors.

CHARLESTON, SOUTH CAROLINA IS A HAVEN FOR WONDERFUL FOODS AND BOLD FLAVORS. The beautiful coast line is home to many hidden jewels for culinary artist to rediscover and recreate for food connoisseurs worldwide. There are so many seafood options to choose from to say the least. I particularly love oysters. The first time I ever had the pleasure of tasting oyster cornbread dressing was during a Thanksgiving holiday when my father introduced it to me. I kind of stood back and watched just after he finished cooking a roaster pan full. I can remember like it was yesterday, the wonderful aroma along with the amazing experience.

SWEET GULLAH OYSTER & SAUSAGE CORNBREAD DRESSING

COOK TIME: 1 HOUR | SERVES: 8

Ingredients

4 Boxes of jiffy cornbread mix

4 Eggs

1 1/3 Cup of milk

2 Sticks of unsalted butter

1 Pound of smoked sausage *(sliced)*

1 Medium yellow onion

1 Large green bell pepper

5 Stalks of celery

1 Tablespoon of ground black pepper

½ Tablespoon of seasoned salt

2 Tablespoons of ground poultry seasoning

1 Tablespoons of sage *(ground or chopped)*

1 Bag of stuffing mix

15 Fresh oysters

1 Quart of turkey or chicken broth

3 Eggs *(beaten)*

Directions

PRE-HEAT THE OVEN TO 400. Prepare the jiffy cornbread according to package directions. In the meantime, place a large skillet on the stove on medium high. Add the sausage, onions, bell pepper, and celery. Sautee until the sausage is cooked for about five minutes or until vegetables are translucent. Remove from the stove and set aside to cool. Remove the cornbread from the oven and set aside to cool. In a large mixing bowl, crumble the cornbread and add all remaining ingredients. Mix well. The dressing shouldn't be dry. If more liquid is needed, broth or milk may be used until the right consistency is reached. The batter should be a little loose. Cover with foil and bake for about an hour. Remove the foil and check to see if the center is set. Once the center is set, remove from the oven and drizzle a little more broth over the top. Enjoy!

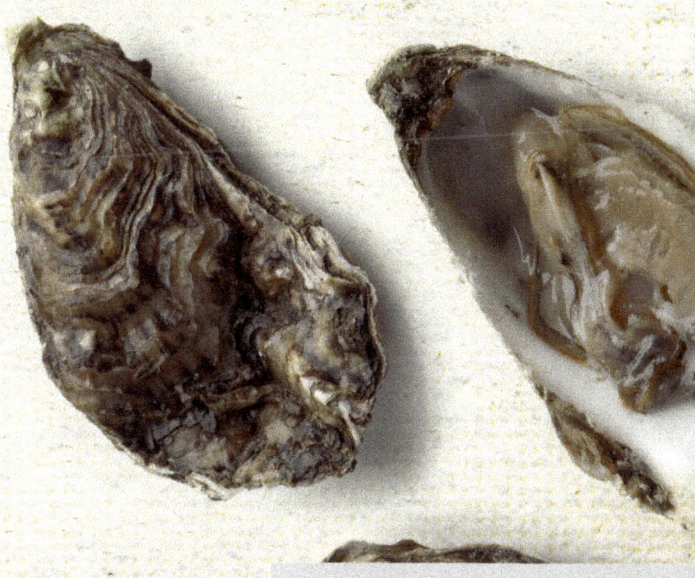

Carolina Soul | 74

Russell's Beer Battered Frog Legs

ONE OF THE THINGS I LOVE ABOUT MY COUSIN RUSSELL IS THAT HE ISN'T AFRAID TO TRY ANYTHING. One Sunday afternoon we got together to watch a little football. He brought over a couple of wonderful ribeye steaks along with some frog legs. I decided to use a beer batter as opposed to the normal buttermilk fried, and it turned out great!

RUSSELL'S BEER BATTERED FROG LEGS

COOK TIME: 6 MINUTES | SERVES: 2

Ingredients

1 ½ Quart of vegetable oil

2 Pounds of frog legs *(whole or split)*

1 ½ Cups of all-purpose flour

1 Teaspoon of Cajon seasoning

1 Teaspoon of garlic powder

1 Teaspoon of onion powder

1 Teaspoon of dry thyme

1 Teaspoon of cayenne pepper

1 Teaspoon of seasoned salt

1 Tablespoon of tbasco sauce

1 Bottle of beer

1 Teaspoon of baking powder

1 Cup of yellow cornmeal

Directions

PREHEAT THE OIL TO 375. Use a deep fryer or cast-iron skillet. Place the frog legs in a bowl and cover with water. Sprinkle about a tablespoon of salt over the frog legs. Allow to thaw for about 30 minutes. In the meantime, add to a mixing bowl the seasonings except for the cornmeal and mix well. Remove the frog legs from the water and place them into the batter. Place in the refrigerator for about an hour. In a separate dish, add the cornmeal. Remove the legs from the refrigerator and pour the frog legs into a strainer and let the batter drain off for about 10 minutes. Place the frog legs into the cornmeal and then immediately place them into the oil. Cook the frog legs for about six minutes while turning once if using a skillet. Do not overcook. Remove from the oil and place onto a paper towel lined pan or platter to drain. Serve with tabasco or Creole mayo. Enjoy

CREOLE MAYONNAISE

SERVINGS VARY

Ingredients

1 ½ Cup of mayonnaise

2 Tablespoons of whole grain mustard

1 Teaspoon of Creole seasoning

½ Tablespoon of lemon juice

2 Tablespoon of green onions *(chopped)*

1 Teaspoon of garlic powder

Pinch of cayenne pepper

Pinch of salt

Pinch of sugar

Pinch of salt

Directions

Combine all the ingredients into a mixing bowl. Mix well. Store in a plastic container with a tight-fitting lid and place into the refrigerator until ready for use.

CAROLINA REMOULADE SAUCE

SERVINGS VARY

Ingredients

1 Cup of mayonnaise

1 ½ Tablespoons of Dijon mustard sauce

1 Tablespoon of tabasco sauce

1 Tablespoon of lemon juice

1 Teaspoon of Worcestershire sauce

1 Shallot *(fine minced)*

2 Cloves of garlic *(fine minced)*

1 Teaspoon of sugar

Pinch of salt

Pinch of crushed red pepper flakes

1 Teaspoon of Cajon seasoning

Directions

In a small mixing bowl, combine all the ingredients and mix well. Place into a small container, cover and refrigerate for at least an hour.

I HAVE A FRIEND NAMED RON WHO LOVES TO COOK AND DOUBLES AS A CLOSET CHEF WHEN NO ONE IS AROUND. I wonder how many meals I've cooked that he's taken credit for. LOL

His mother is a terrific cook and I've had the privilege of cooking for many of their family events and celebrations. I must always bring my "A" game because as a family, they have a few tricks in the kitchen of their own. So, one day I was in Charlotte at Ron's house preparing to whip up a meal, while looking over the menu, I suggested we switch up a couple of the items. The greens were always good, but I recalled a few times where my Aunt Gladys would mix her collard greens together with cabbage. I have to say it was pretty good. Laced with smoked turkey and just the right amount of heat, this combination was phenomenal!

It is very important to make sure the greens are fresh. Whether you pick the greens yourself or buy the prepackaged type, they need to be fresh and washed thoroughly. While some stem is needed for that wonderful pot liquor, too much is not good. I like to take the time to get my greens cup and put into the sink. I run cold water over the greens until there's just enough water to cover them. Then, I sprinkle salt over the greens. This isn't a way to season the greens, but rather a way to pull out all the impurities, dirt, and grit away from the greens. If you've ever had a mouth full of greens that weren't washed well, you know exactly what I'm talking about. It's not a pleasant experience. In my family, we will talk about you for terrible greens. As a matter of fact, anybody who loves collard greens, mustard greens, turnips greens etc. If your greens are bad, we are talking about you to your faced and behind your back.

I grew up thinking that the only meat to put in "greens" were ham hocks. However, smoked ham hocks, neck bones, smoked pig tails and even pig ears can be used as well. Anything that would add the "smokiness "to the greens, as my mother would say so with profundity! My Aunt Jan had the best greens ever. She would always add some grease that she used to fry chicken in the greens. The grease had so much flavor, it's a tradition that has carried on from generation to generation. Of course, there are those of us who may not want any meat in their greens, so therefore the question always comes up, how can I add flavor without the meat? You can use liquid smoke, a good homemade veggie broth, and other natural seasoning, garlic powder, seasoning salt and crushed red pepper are other alternatives for a "meaty taste" without the meat. I used smoke turkey for this particular recipe. Hope you enjoy!

> It is **very important** to make sure the
> **GREENS ARE FRESH.**

RON'S COLLARDS AND CABBAGE

COOK TIME: 1 HOUR AND 20 MINUTES | **SERVES:** 10

Ingredients

½ Gallon of chicken broth or water

2 Packages of Saizon seasoning *(chicken flavor)*

2 Smoked turkey legs or wings

1 Teaspoon of crushed red pepper flakes

1 Large onion chopped

2 Pounds of fresh collard greens *(washed well, chopped or cut into 2-inch pieces)*

1 Tablespoon of garlic powder

2 Teaspoons of ground black pepper

2 Tablespoons of seasoned salt

2 Teaspoons of sugar *(if the greens are bitter)*

1 Head of cabbage *(chopped or cut into 2-inch pieces)*

Directions

Place a 10-quart stockpot onto the stove on high. Add the seasoning pack and smoked turkey into the pot along with the crushed red pepper flakes. Allow the pot to come to a boil. Place a lid on the pot and reduce the heat to medium low and allow to cook for about one hour or until the meat is fork tender. Add the onions, collards, garlic powder, black pepper, and seasoned salt. Continue to cook for about 1 hour or until the greens are tender. Sample the greens. If the greens are a little bitter, add a couple of teaspoons of sugar. Add the cabbage to the greens and continue cooking for an additional 20 minutes. Adjust the flavors according to your taste. Add hot pepper sauce or cayenne for more spice if desired. Can be served with cornbread. Enjoy!

SPOTS are a seasonal fish that typically runs from August through October.

MY FRIEND CHRIS WILCOX IS A FAN OF FRIED SPOTS. Every summer we would sit around talking about football and whose team is going to be garbage in the coming fall. Somehow the conversation would turn to "fish," fried fish in particular and "spots." Sure enough, Chris and I along with Rell, Chuck, and the rest of the fellas would laugh as we take turns shooting pool and sipping Coronas. Spots are a seasonal fish that typically runs from August through October. When you hear the phrase "their running," that means the spots are running and it's time to hit the fishing bank or one of the many large rivers in the Carolina regions.

GOLDEN FRIED SPOTS

COOK TIME: 8 MINUTES | SERVINGS VARY

Ingredients

2 Pounds of spots *(scaled, gutted, and washed well in cold water)*

3 Cups of vegetable oil

2 Cups of yellow corn meal

½ Tablespoon of coarse black pepper

1 Tablespoon of salt

Directions

Place a cast iron skillet on the stove on medium high heat. Add the oil and allow it to come up to a temperature of 350 degrees. In the meantime, in a mixing bowl, combine the corn meal, pepper and salt. Mix well. Coat the fresh fish in the cornmeal mixture and immediately place into the oil. Do not over crowd the pan. Cook for about 4 minutes on each side or until the fish is flaky. Remove from the skillet and place on a paper towel lined platter. Drain well and enjoy. Personally, all I need is bread and hot sauce for this. Well maybe a nice cold Corona. Enjoy!

Eno River
Durham, North Carolina

BEANS ARE AN OLD FAVORITE OF THE CAROLINAS. It's a very inexpensive food item, in addition beans are very healthy. Beans have an overabundance of iron, fiber, potassium, zinc, along with antioxidants. In fact, beans are known to decrease the risk of diabetes, heart disease, and colon cancer.

I'm not a bean fan. Perhaps, because my siblings and I ate so many while I was growing up. It got to the point where there was a series of weeks that went by where it seemed as if that was all we were eating. I vowed to never eat beans again once I was grown and on my own. As I looked back on those days, I realize momma was doing whatever she had to do to get by. Regardless of how many beans we ate, if you didn't want to go hungry, you would eat those beans. Besides that, we couldn't get up from the table until the beans were gone. I tried to trick my sister Tricia a time or two by offering her my beans if she would give me her fried chicken. It worked the first two times. After that, she wasn't falling for it.

Now that I'm older and have acquired a different taste and use for a variety of beans, I'm able to enjoy and share my ideas with the rest of the world. There's nothing like a good chili. Especially with great northern beans. This recipe is a nod to my sister Tricia who not only makes a great chili of her own but is a true bean lover.

GREAT NORTHERN CAROLINA CHILI

COOK TIME: 45 MINUTES | SERVES: 8

Ingredients

4 Strips of bacon *(sliced)*

1 Yellow onion *(diced)*

1 Pound each of diced chicken breast and boneless thighs

Pinch of crushed red pepper flakes

1 Teaspoon of dry thyme

1 Tablespoon of seasoned salt

1 Teaspoon of white pepper

1 Tablespoon of rotisserie seasoning

1 Tablespoon of minced garlic

3 Tablespoons of fresh chopped parsley

4 Cans of great northern beans

3 Cups of chicken broth

Directions

Place a 5-quart pot on the stove on medium high. Add the bacon and sauté for about four minutes or until the bacon is done. Remove the bacon and set aside for garnish. Add the onions, chicken, pepper flakes, thyme, salt, pepper, rotisserie seasoning, and garlic. Continue to cook for about 5 minutes. Continue to stir to prevent sticking. Add the remaining ingredients and bring to a boil. Cover with a lid and reduce the heat to simmer. Cook for about 45 minutes. Spoon into a bowl or serving dish and garnish with the bacon. Enjoy!

GOOD BBQ AND GREAT SAUCES ARE WORLDWIDE ACCOLADES OF BOTH CAROLINAS. While eastern North Carolina is known for its vinegar based sauce, South Carolina is known for the mustard based sauce. I love the taste of them both.

Back in 2016 I had the wonderful opportunity to experience and compete in the largest food sport in the world known as the World Food Championship. There were a myriad of categories of food, coupled with the top one thousand chefs in the world gearing up to battle it out to see which teams would end up in the top ten. I began to wander about to check out the competition. My nose led me over to trail of smoke coming from a group of trailers. It was there I discovered the wonderful South Carolina approach to BBQ. I remember the kind gentleman talking about his personal approach to BBQ. He said "the only way to have good BBQ is to have good patience. You've got to go slow and low. You can't rush it. And another thing, the sauce is key. I don't know what the hell they doing everywhere else, but down in South Carolina, we do it right. It's the mustard base that reigns supreme!"

I say to each his own. But, that South Carolina style BBQ sauce is amazing when it's done right. I came up with my own version and I think it's pretty good. Here's to the Palmetto State and the wonderful mustard based BBQ sauce.

SOUTH CAROLINA BBQ SAUCE

COOK TIME: 20 MINUTES | SERVINGS VARY

Ingredients

1 Cup of white vinegar

½ Cup of sugar

½ Cup of lite brown sugar

1 Teaspoon of crushed red pepper flakes

1 Cup of honey

2 Cups of yellow mustard

2 Teaspoons of dry mustard

1/3 Cup of hot sauce

2 Tablespoons of Worcestershire sauce

Directions

Place a small saucepan on the stove over medium heat. Add the vinegar, sugars, and honey. Stir well. Continue to cook and stir until the sugars are dissolved. Add the remaining ingredients and mix well. Continue to cook for about 20 minutes. Taste and adjust flavors to your desire. Enjoy!

THIS WONDERFUL RICE DISH WAS ORIGINALLY A MEAL THAT WAS BROUGHT OVER TO AMERICA BY SLAVES FROM THE WEST COAST OF AFRICA. This dish is so full of bold flavors consisting of fresh herbs and tomatoes, and is almost always complimented with some sort of pork flavoring. That's if you want to keep it authentic in your approach. However, smoked turkey will make for a great substitute. This dish is synonymous with the Gullah or Geechee people and heritage.

This dish is so *full of bold flavors* consisting of **FRESH HERBS** and **TOMATOES,** and is almost always complimented with some sort of *pork flavoring.*

CHARLESTON RED RICE

COOK TIME: 45 MINUTES | SERVES: 10

Ingredients

- 5 Slices of bacon
- ½ Pound of spicy ground pork sausage
- 2 Yellow onions *(chopped)*
- Pinch of crushed red pepper flakes
- 1 Teaspoon of curry powder
- 1 Bay leaf
- 1 (8 ounce) can of tomato sauce
- 1 (6 ounce) can of tomato paste
- 1 Large diced tomato
- 1 Tablespoon of sugar
- 1 Tablespoon of Worcestershire sauce
- ¼ Cup of hot sauce
- 2 Cups of long grain white rice
- 6 Cups of chicken broth

Directions

PREHEAT THE OVEN TO 425. Place a large skillet on the stove on medium high. Slice or chop the bacon and add it to the skillet. Once the bacon is done, remove it from the pan and place on a paper towel to drain. Do not remove the bacon grease. Add the sausage, onions, red pepper, and curry powder. Sautee for about 5 minutes. Add the tomato sauce and paste along with the sugar. Stir well. Add the remaining ingredients along with the bacon and stir well. Transfer the entire dish to a 2-quart baking dish. Cover tightly with foil and place in the oven for about 45 minutes. Check the rice and give a good stir. Serve as a wonderful side to your meal. Enjoy!

MY MOTHER HAD A WAY OF MAKING EVERYTHING SEEM "OK" METAPHORICALLY WITH HER COOKING. It didn't matter what it was. That's what comfort food does. It has a way of removing every worry and instantaneously dissipating stress. Her boiled chicken and egg noodle recipe remains one of my favorites until this very day. It's the perfect simple, quick and easy meal. When it's raining and snowing, this dish is perfect for "sticking to the bones" as we say in the south. This is the kind of meal that will make you curl up on the sofa and sleep like a baby.

KATHERINE'S BOILED CHICKEN AND NOODLES

COOK TIME: 1 HOUR AND 10 MINUTES | SERVES: 4

Ingredients

1 Whole chicken

2 Quarts of chicken broth

1 Yellow or white onion

Pinch of crushed red pepper flakes

4 Celery stalks *(chopped)*

½ Tablespoon of dry thyme

6 Cloves of crushed garlic

2 Tablespoons of seasoned salt

1 Tablespoon of coarse black pepper

1 Stick of butter

1 Bag of egg noodles

Directions

Place a 2 ½ quart pot onto the stove on medium high. Place the chicken and the broth into the pot and bring to a boil. Add the onion, pepper flakes, celery, thyme, garlic, seasoned salt, and pepper. Cover with a lid and reduce the heat to simmer. Cook for about an hour or until the chicken comes off the bone. Add the butter and noodles. Cook for 10 minutes or until the noodles are tender. Spoon into a bowl and enjoy. Enjoy!

SOUTHERN VEGGIE BITES

COOK TIME: **6** MINUTES | SERVES: **4**

Ingredients

2 ½ Cups of vegetable oil

1 Pound of broccoli crowns

1 Pound of cauliflower crowns

2 Cups of all-purpose flour

1 Bottle of beer

1 Tablespoon of rotisserie seasoning

1 Pinch of crushed red pepper flakes

1 Tablespoon of garlic powder

1 Tablespoon of seasoned salt

2 Teaspoons of baking powder

Directions

Place a 1-quart sauce pot on the stove on medium high. Add the oil to the pot and bring the temperature to 350. Place a 2-quart pot onto the stove and fill halfway with water. Bring to a boil. Add the vegetables and reduce to medium low. Cook the vegetables for about 3 minutes. Remove the vegetables from the stove and place into a strainer. Run cold water over the vegetables or place the vegetables into ice water to stop the cooking. Once the vegetables are cool, allow them to drain well.

In a mixing bowl, combine the flour, beer, and seasonings. Mix well and allow to sit for about 10 minutes. Place the vegetables into the batter and immediately place a few into the oil. Cook for about 3 minutes or until golden brown. Remove the vegetables from the oil and place on a paper towel to soak up the oil. Repeat the cooking steps until all the vegetables are cooked. Serve as a side to your favorite meal. Enjoy!

PAN FRIED GRIT CAKES

COOK TIME: 50 MINUTES | SERVES: 4

Ingredients

2 Cups of water

½ Stick up salted butter

6 ½ Tablespoons of quick grits

2 Teaspoons of garlic powder

1 Small red bell pepper *(minced)*

2 Stalks of green onions *(chopped)*

1 Teaspoon of black pepper

1/3 Cup of grated parmesan cheese

1 Tablespoon of Mascarpone cheese

28x18x4 Pyrex pan

Parchment paper

1 Cup of vegetable oil

1 ½ Cup of all-purpose flour

2 eggs

1 ½ Cup of milk or water

1 ½ Cup of Italian bread crumbs

Directions

Place a small sauce pot on the stove on the stove on high. Add the water, and butter. Bring the water to a boil. While stirring with a whisk, add the grits and continue to stir for about one minute. Cover with a lid and reduce the heat to simmer. Continue to cook for about 5 minutes. Stir occasionally. Once the grits are done, add the remaining ingredients and stir well. Remove the pot from the stove and pour into a parchment lined Pyrex pan. Cover with plastic wrap and place the pan in the refrigerator. Allow the grits to completely cool.

Place a large skillet onto the stove on medium high. Pour the oil in the pan and allow the temperature to heat to 325 degrees. Then, combine the eggs and milk and mix well until well blended. Cut the grits into a desired shape. Place the grit cake into the flour. Shake off the excess. Dip the cake into the egg mixture and then into the Italian bread crumbs. Place the grits cake into the oil. Cook for 2 ½ minutes on each side. Transfer to a paper towel lined pan to drain. Enjoy!

SAUTÉED BRUSSELS SPROUTS
TOSSED IN GARLIC BUTTER GLAZE

COOK TIME: **10** MINUTES | SERVES: **4**

Ingredients

2 Pounds of Brussels sprouts *(washed, split in half)*

3 Cups of chicken broth

Pinch of Kosher salt

1 Tablespoon of seasoned salt

1 Teaspoon of black pepper

3 Strips of chopped bacon

1 Shallot *(chopped)*

1 Teaspoon of garlic powder

½ Tablespoon of minced garlic

1 Teaspoon of sugar

½ Stick of unsalted butter

¼ Cup of heavy cream

Directions

Place a 2 ½ quart sauce pot on the stove on high. Add the broth to the pot and bring it to a boil. Place the sprouts into the pot and cover with a lid. Allow the sprouts to cook for about 3 minutes. Once the sprouts are cooked, place them into a bowl filled with ice-water to stop the cooking process. Once the sprouts are cold, remove from the water and drain well on a paper towel.

Place a large skillet onto the stove on medium high. Add the bacon, shallot, and garlic powder to the pan and cook until the bacon is done. Add the sprouts and the remaining ingredients to the skillet and mix well. Reduce the heat to medium low and continue to cook until the sauce has thickened. Enjoy!

CHEF ROME'S
CAROLINA STYLE FRENCH TOAST FINISHED WITH D'USSE COGNAC SYRUP

COOK TIME: 10 MINUTES | SERVES: 10

Ingredients

SYRUP

1 Stick of butter

½ Cup of brown sugar

½ Cup of white sugar

1 Tablespoon of vanilla extract

2 Cups of D'usse cognac liqueur

FRENCH TOAST

1 Loaf of French bread *(sliced into 1½ inch pieces)*

2 Cups of milk

2 Eggs *(beaten well)*

¼ Cup of sugar

1 Tablespoon of vanilla extract

¼ Cup of grand Marnier

2 Sticks of salted butter

Powdered sugar for garnish

Directions

Place a 2-quart sauce pot onto the stove on medium high. Place the butter, and sugars into the pot and mix well until smooth. Add the remaining ingredients and mix well. Reduce the heat to simmer. Continue to allow the syrup to cook for an additional 15 minutes or until desired thickness is reached, stirring occasionally. Set aside until ready to use. Store in a plastic container or glass jar with a tight-fitting lid. Store in the refrigerator and reheat when ready for use.

Place a large skillet on the stove on medium high. In a large bowl, combine the milk and eggs. Mix well until the eggs are well beaten. Add the sugar, vanilla, and grand Marnier. Soak the bread into the batter for about 3-5 minutes. Add the butter to the skillet and allow the butter to melt. Remove the bread from the batter and place into the skillet. Cook for about 2 ½ minutes on each side. Place the toast onto a skillet or plate. Sprinkle with powdered sugar. Pour over the desired syrup. Enjoy!

I'M NOT 100% SURE HOW TASTE OF PARADISE OF ROCKY MOUNT PREPARES THEIR OXTAILS, HOWEVER, WHEN I SPEAK TO SOME OF MY CLOSEST JAMAICAN FRIENDS, I END UP WITH A FEW VARIATIONS AS TO HOW THIS WONDERFUL DISH SHOULD BE PREPARED AND SERVED. This dish is prepared by a cooking method called braising. Follow the steps and you will have a new family favorite.

JAMAICAN OXTAIL STEW

COOK TIME: 3 HOURS | SERVES: 5

Ingredients

3 Pounds of oxtails
(trim about half the fat)

½ Cup of vegetable oil

1 ½ Cup of all-purpose flour

1 Tablespoon of all spice

1 Tablespoon of seasoned salt

½ Tablespoon of salt

½ Tablespoon of coarse black pepper

1 Tablespoon of garlic powder

2 Bay leaves

4 Sprigs of fresh thyme

1 Large onion *(yellow or white)*

1 Scotch bonnet pepper *(sliced)*
(use rubber gloves)

½ Cup of Worcestershire sauce

4 Roma tomatoes *(large diced)*

2 Cups of dried baby lima beans
(quick soak method)

5 Cups of beef broth

Directions

PREHEAT THE OVEN TO 325 DEGREES. Place a large skillet or heavy bottom pot onto the stove on medium high. Add the oil to the pan. In a bowl, combine the flour, salt and pepper. Mix well. Coat the oxtails in the flour. Shake off the excess and place into the oil. Brown on all sides. Add more oil if needed. Once the oxtails are browned on all sides, add them to a roaster pan. Then, add the remaining ingredients to the roaster as well. Cover with foil and a tight-fitting lid. Place the roaster into the oven and allow the oxtails to cook for about three hours or until fork tender. Remove the roaster from the oven and serve over rice and peas or my favorite Jasmine saffron rice. Enjoy!

I LOVE JASMINE RICE. Not because it just so happens to be my daughter's name but it's truly one of the great side dishes for any wonderful meal. It can be served plain or with Jamaican oxtails or even with seafood. My son Joshua, makes a baked fish that pairs well with this rice. It's quick, simple, and easy. Those are the three favorite words that most cooks all over the world can appreciate.

JASMINE SAFFRON COCONUT RICE

COOK TIME: 12 - 15 MINUTES | SERVES: 4

Ingredients

3 Cup of chicken or vegetable broth

1 can of coconut milk

2 Cup of Jasmine rice

1 Teaspoon of Kosher salt

1 Bay leaf

Pinch of saffron

2 Tablespoons of unsalted butter

Directions

Rinse the rice under cold water and drain well. Place a sauce pot onto the stove on high. Add to the pot the broth, coconut milk, and salt. Mix well and bring to a boil. Stir in the rice, bay leaf, and saffron. Cover with a tight-fitting lid. Reduce the heat to low and continue to cook for about 15 minutes. Remove the pot from the heat and let it stand for about 10 minutes. Add the butter and lightly fluff with a fork and serve immediately. I recommend this dish with my oxtail recipe. Enjoy!

I HAD NEVER HEARD OF DIRTY RICE UNTIL MY MOTHER RELOCATED BACK TO NORTH CAROLINA FROM OHIO. I remember thinking, *What's so dirty about it?* Traditionally it's a Cajun and Creole dish made from white rice, chicken livers, and gizzards as the primary ingredients. During my time of working for Shaquille O'Neal, D Mac's parents were visiting form New Orleans. When I told his mom, what was on the menu for the evening, she asked me if I knew what I was doing. I said "yes." She asked, "What goes in your dirty rice?" When I told her, she looked at me sideways. She grabbed a piece of paper and said, "Go to the store and grab these ingredients for me." That night, I had the best dirty rice of my life. She, as we say down south, "put her foot in it," it was absolutely amazing. Shaq's mom schooled me that night!

THE DIRTIEST RICE

COOK TIME: 50 MINUTES | SERVES: 10

Ingredients

1 Pound of chicken livers

½ Pound of chicken gizzards

1 Pound of ground pork sausage

1 Pound of ground beef

1 Large yellow onion *(diced)*

1 Green bell pepper *(diced)*

1 Red bell pepper *(diced)*

2 Stalks of celery *(diced)*

1 Bunch of scallions *(thin sliced)*

2 Tablespoons of minced garlic

2 Bay leaves

1 Tablespoon of cayenne pepper

1 Tablespoon of seasoned salt
(or "slap Ya Mammas Seasoning")

2 Cups of long grain white rice
(rinsed under cold water and drained well)

2 Cups each of chicken and beef broth

½ Cup of Worcestershire sauce

1 Cup of fresh Italian parsley

Directions

Place a two-quart pot onto the stove on high. Add the livers and gizzards to the pot and cover with water. Bring to a boil. Cook for about 20 minutes. Remove the livers and gizzards and place in a small bowl and allow to cool. Reserve the liquid for later use. Once the livers and gizzards are cool. Chop well. Place a large saucepan or Dutch oven pot onto the stove on medium high. Add the sausage and beef. Sautee' for about 5 minutes. Add the liver, gizzards, onions, bell peppers and celery. Continue to cook until the vegetables have softened. Add the remaining ingredients and mix well. Cover with a tight-fitting lid. Reduce the heat to simmer and cook for about 30 minutes. Turn off the heat and let stand for about 10 additional minutes. Next, fluff with a fork! Enjoy!

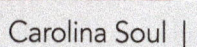

I CAN'T BELIEVE I WAS IN MY LATE 40'S BEFORE I TRIED MY FIRST PO BOY. I know, I know. Where's the rock I was hiding under? I hadn't heard of a Po Boy until I was walking along the streets of Charleston, South Carolina and stumbled upon a phenomenal restaurant called Hyman's Seafood. I love my vegetables and I figured it was a great time to try the fried green tomato Po Boy. I put down my carnivorous appetite just temporarily but ended up adding the crawfish tails. It was awesome! The key to a great Po Boy is to serve it in a fresh baguette.

FRIED GREEN TOMATO PO BOY WITH CRAWFISH REMOULADE

COOK TIME: 8 - 10 MINUTES | **SERVES:** 2

Ingredients

2 Cups of vegetable oil

2 Green tomatoes
(sliced ¼ - ½ inch thick)

Salt and Pepper to taste

1 Tablespoon of garlic powder

1 Cup of all-purpose flour

1 Cup of buttermilk

2 Eggs *(beaten)*

2 Tablespoons of tabasco sauce

1 ½ Cup of Panko bread crumbs

2 Tablespoons of Italian seasoning

2 Six-inch baguette rolls *(fresh)*

½ Cup of chopped crawfish tails
(chopped)

½ Cup of remoulade sauce

1 Cup of shredded lettuce

Directions

Place a large skillet onto the stove on medium high. Add the oil. Let the oil heat up while preparing the remaining ingredients. Slice the tomatoes and set aside on a paper towel lined sheet pan. Season each slice with the salt, pepper, and garlic on both sides.

Place three bowls on the table. In the first bowl add the flour. In the second bowl, add the buttermilk, eggs, and tabasco sauce. Mix well. In the third bowl, add the bread crumbs and Italian seasoning. Dip the tomatoes into the flour. Coat well and shake off the excess flour. Place the tomatoes into the buttermilk mixture. Coat well and place into the bread crumbs. Immediately place into the oil. Fry on both sides for about 4 minutes each. Drain well on a paper towel lined sheet pan. Butter the rolls and place face side down until golden brown. Combine the crawfish with the remoulade sauce. Add the sauce to the roll and then the lettuce. Top with the tomatoes. Enjoy!

I HAVE 12 NEPHEWS, I LOVE ANY OPPORTUNITY TO HEAR ABOUT THEIR ACCOMPLISHMENTS BUT I AM ALSO IMPRESSED BY THEIR COOKING. All the men in my family can cook for the most part. But there are some who really aspire to perfect that one special dish that makes us eat like gluttons when we get together. Of course, we brag about who can do it the best or who makes the best whatever. But I say, if we all bring something to the table, we can all eat well. My nephew Quan has some pretty good ribs. I've asked him for the recipe about 50 times or so and he still hasn't given it to me yet. But through the power of a trained tongue for food, I think I have it figured out.

I have 12 nephews, *I love any opportunity to hear about their accomplishments* but I am also **IMPRESSED BY THEIR COOKING.**

QUAN'S RIBS

COOK TIME: 1 HOUR AND 20 MINUTES | SERVINGS VARY

Ingredients

3 Slabs of baby back ribs *(rinsed, patted dry, trimmed of any excess fat)*

1 Cup of vegetable oil

1 Cup of seasoned salt

1 Tablespoon of coarse black pepper

1 Tablespoon of garlic powder

1 Tablespoon of brown sugar

½ Tablespoon of chili powder

Directions

Pre-heat the oven to 350. In a medium size bowl, combine all the ingredients and mix well. Rub all over the ribs. Wrap the ribs in plastic wrap and place into the refrigerator overnight.

Prepare your grill. Spray the rack with non-stick cooking spray. Once the coals have died down and have reached a temperature of about 200 degrees, your ribs are ready to go on the grill. Use a meat thermometer to assist with arriving at the perfect temperature. Place the ribs on the grill. Do not overcrowd. Close the lid and let the ribs cook for about 20 minutes and then turn over and cook on the other side for 20 minutes. Remove the ribs from the grill and place into a roaster. Add a cup of water to the bottom of the pan. Cover with foil and place into the oven for about an hour.

Remove from the over. Let the ribs sit for about 15 minutes. Add sauce to the ribs or serve on the side. Enjoy!

LIMA BEANS ARE ONE OF TWO BEANS THAT I DON'T MIND EATING. As I said before, my mother fed us so many beans as I was growing up that I actually went years as an adult without eating them. The lima bean is more of a "creamy bean." There's a natural sweetness to this bean that comes out through the cooking process. Add a little butter and cream along with some smoked meat and you really have a great meal.

MAMMA'S BABY LIMA AND SHRIMP

COOK TIME: **33** MINUTES | SERVES: **4**

Ingredients

2 Pounds of baby lima beans *(shelled and washed under cold water)*

2 Strips of bacon

½ Small onion (chopped)

2 Tablespoons of unsalted butter

1 Teaspoon of black pepper

1 Teaspoon of garlic powder

1 Teaspoon of sugar

½ Pound of popcorn shrimp

½ Cup of heavy cream or half and half

Directions

Place the beans in a sauce pot with enough water to cover. Bring the beans to a boil and cover with a lid. Reduce the heat to simmer. Cook for about 30 minutes. Drain the beans and set aside momentarily.

Place a large skillet on the stove on medium high. Add the bacon and onion to the skillet and cook until the bacon is done but not burnt. Add the butter, beans, pepper, garlic, and sugar. Continue to cook for about two minutes. Add the shrimp and the cream. Continue to cook for about three additional minutes. Enjoy!

AS OF 2017 THE STATE OF NORTH CAROLINA HAS OPENED IT'S WATER WAYS UP FOR BAY SCALLOP HARVEST. That's great news for scallop lovers like myself who enjoy visiting places like Topsail Sound! For several years, fisherman were not allowed to go out and harvest bay scallops due to the state regulated restrictions. But it's a new day! I'm getting my favorite recipes ready.

LINGUINI AND BAY SCALLOPS
TOSSED IN LEMON BUTTER SAUCE

COOK TIME: 5 MINUTES | **SERVES:** 4

Ingredients

1 Pound of linguini *(cooked according to package directions)*

3 Pounds of bay scallops

2 Tablespoons of olive oil

½ Cup of melted butter

½ Cup of blackening seasoning

4 Cloves of garlic *(sliced)*

Juice of one lemon

¼ Cup of fresh grated parmesan cheese

¼ Cup of fresh flat leaf parsley *(chopped)*

Directions

Place a large cast iron skillet on the stove over medium high. Combine the olive oil and the melted butter. Mix well. Place the scallops in the oils. Use a mixing bowl to toss the oiled scallops into the blackening seasoning. Once the skillet is hot, place the scallops into the skillet and cook for about 1 ½ minutes on each side. Add the garlic, and continue to sauté. Add the cooked pasta, lemon juice, parmesan, and parsley. Toss well and serve immediately. Enjoy!

Wild Berry Skillet

OVER THE CHRISTMAS HOLIDAYS I WAS SITTING AROUND TALKING TO MY SON JOSHUA AND MY SECOND DAUGHTER LEONI. Talk about a mistake that turned into a delicious dessert? Those two came up with a disastrously yummy surprise that we continue to laugh about even to this day. This dessert has all the wonderful components that anyone who enjoys sweets will be sure to appreciate. Joshua has always had a sweet tooth. It started with him bribing Leoni to let him drive to the store. Joshua has absolutely no driver's license whatsoever. That was a mistake. We had a conversation about that. Anyway, he purchased ingredients thinking he was going to make a pie. It went left after that! He needed help with the filling. Leoni being the aspiring pastry chef that she is, pitched in with a helping hand. She noticed that her brother was struggling, so he said. "Whatever he did to the filling, it was runny." So, their first task was to figure out how to thicken it up. Then, Leoni suggested that he let the filling reduce during the cooking process. That didn't work at all. Somehow that turned into adding a flour and a water paste. His impatience was getting the best of him so they both decided to add a custard and a meringue. Somehow this so-called pie was turning into an entirely different tasty dessert.

WILD BERRY SKILLET

COOK TIME: 45 MINUTES | SERVINGS VARY

Ingredients

CRUST

1 ½ Cups of graham cracker crumbs

1/3 Cup of sugar

6 Tablespoons of melted butter (unsalted)

Pinch of fresh nutmeg

FILLING

1½ Cup of sliced strawberries

½ Cup of black berries

½ Cup of raspberries

½ Cup of blueberries

½ Cup of sugar

2 Teaspoons of lemon juice

3 Tablespoon of cornstarch

TOPPING

¼ Cup of white sugar

¼ Cup of light corn syrup

3 Tablespoons of water

2 Teaspoons of vanilla extract

1/8 Teaspoon of cream of tarter

Pinch of salt

2 Egg whites

Directions

PRE-HEAT THE OVEN TO 350. In a bowl, combine the graham crackers, sugar and butter. Place a 10-inch cast iron skillet onto the counter. Add the graham cracker mixture into the skillet. Press on all sides until evenly distributed. Place in the oven and bake for about 8 minutes. Remove from the oven and let it cool for about an hour. Raise the oven temperature to 400 degrees. In the same bowl, combine the berries, sugar, lemon juice, and cornstarch. Mix well. Add the berry mixture to the crust. Place into the oven and bake for about 45 minutes. Remove from the oven and let it cool completely.

In a small saucepan, combine the sugar, corn syrup, water, vanilla, cream of tartar, and salt. Place the pan onto the stove on medium high. Stir until all the sugar has dissolved. Remove the pot from the heat and set aside for later use. In a medium bowl, beat the egg whites until foamy on medium speed. Once the egg whites are foamy, add to sugar mixture.

Turn the speed up to high and continue mixing until stiff peaks form. Do not over mix. Spread the meringue over the pie mixture.

NOTE: *If you choose to brown the meringue, you may place into the over until the desired color is reached or use a food torch. Enjoy!*

IF YOU'RE FROM THE CAROLINAS, YOU KNOW RED FISH OR AS I CALL IT, "RED DRUM." This fish is mild in flavor and has very little oil. I came up with a simple recipe that yields a very good flavor when not overcooked. Grilling is a wonderful way to prepare this fish with the seasonings and smoke flavors added.

GRILLED RED DRUM

COOK TIME: 12 - 15 MINUTES | **SERVES:** 6

Ingredients

2 Pounds of fresh red fish

¼ Cup of olive oil

Juice of one lemon

½ Cup of melted butter *(unsalted)*

1 Teaspoon of cayenne pepper

1 Teaspoon of paprika

2 Teaspoons of chopped garlic

1 Tablespoon of seasoned salt

Directions

Prepare the grill by spraying non-stick evenly over the rack. Light the grill. In the meantime, remove all scales and rinse well under cold water. Use a paper towel to pat the fish dry. Coat the skin side of the fish with olive oil. Turn the fish over and season the inside with the lemon juice, butter, cayenne pepper, paprika, garlic, and salt. Place the fish onto the grill flesh side down. Allow to cook for about 5 minutes. Use two spatulas to turn the fish over. Allow the fish to continue to cook for an additional 7 minutes or until the fish is flakey. Be careful not to overcook the fish. Remove the fish from the grill to a platter. Enjoy!

I WILL NEVER FORGET THE TIME I WENT INTO ONE OF THE LOCAL CORNER STORES IN SOUTH ROCKY MOUNT. My family had just relocated from Ohio back to NC. I saw a sign that read, Bologna burger $5.00! I was in shock, was there such a thing? The next day I asked my new friend Shelley had she heard of it. She answered "of course!" In fact, she's the reason I even put this dish in my cookbook. Even though I had eaten this same sandwich many times at home, I just didn't expect to see it sold in a local store. As a latchkey kid, that's what we ate in the morning. A breakfast to go sandwich everyday growing up. Even coming home from school in the afternoon a quick bologna sandwich was a treat. The bologna I loved the most was the welfare bologna. The one with the red string around each slice. OHHHHHH, that was the one! You weren't eating good bologna if you weren't eating the one with the red string. The meat left on that red string wasn't missed on me either. I would put the whole string in my mouth and would eat all of the residue from the string as well. Once I became a chef, I "got fancy" by adding a slice of cheese to it, then I upgraded and grilled it in a cast iron skillet. That's good eating!

OPEN FACE BOLOGNA & EGG SANDWICH

COOK TIME: 5 MINUTES | SERVES: 4

Ingredients

2 English muffins *(split in half)*

1 Stick of unsalted butter

8 Slices of bologna

4 Eggs

Cheese *(optional)*

Directions

Put the muffins into the toaster and cook until desired toasting. Place a skillet onto the stove on medium high. Add about a third of the butter to the pan and melt. Place the slices of bacon into the skillet and cook for about 5 minutes. Turn over once.

Once the bologna is cooked, remove from the pan and cook each egg individually. Add more butter if necessary. Remove the muffins from the toaster. Place two slices of bologna onto the muffin. Top with the egg! (Serves 4) Enjoy!

NOTE: Of course, the good old sliced bread will work just fine.

I LOVE THE MANY WONDERFUL CAULIFLOWER DISHES I'VE SEEN OVER THE LAST FEW YEARS. Of course, chefs are using the various cauliflower plant in a million diverse ways. Cauliflower is a part of the cabbage family and is a great source of vitamin C and Iron. This recipe is made up of a tasty and creamy cheese sauce, then baked to a golden hue akin to macaroni and cheese.

BAKED CREAMY CAULIFLOWER

COOK TIME: **35** MINUTES | SERVES: **4**

Ingredients

1 Quart of vegetable or chicken stock

1 Head of cauliflower *(crowns only)*

1 Tablespoon of seasoned salt

1 Teaspoon of white pepper

½ Tablespoon of garlic powder

1 Cup of heavy cream

¼ Cup of all-purpose flour

¼ Cup of cold water

½ Cup of gruyere cheese

½ Cup of grated sharp cheddar cheese

1 Cup of panko bread crumbs

Pinch of nutmeg

2 Tablespoons of melted butter

Directions

PRE-HEAT THE OVEN TO 400. Butter a shallow 2-quart baking dish. Add the stock to a gallon size pot. Allow the stock to come to a full boil. Next, add the cauliflower crowns to the stock then reduce the heat to medium low. Cook for about 5-6 minutes. Next, remove the pot to a cool part of the stove. Remove the cauliflower from the pot, but do not discard the stock. Place the cauliflower into the baking dish. Add the pepper, garlic powder, and cream to the stock. Return the stock to the stove on medium high.

In a small bowl, combine the flour and water together. Mix well until no lumps remain. While stirring with a whisk, add the flour mixture to the stock. Mix well until smooth. Stir in the cheeses. Mix well. Move the pot to a cool part of the stove or counter. Spoon the cheese sauce over the cauliflower.

In a small bowl, combine the breadcrumbs, nutmeg, and butter. Sprinkle over the cauliflower and bake for about 30 minutes. Remove from the oven and enjoy!

I LOVE DEVILED EGGS! But, it was my dad who introduced me to doing something different with them. Last year on labor day, my sister Linda put so much onion in the deviled eggs that they tasted like potato salad.

I remember getting into trouble in my home economics class in middle school. I attended Catholic school, and this one particular nun was talking about boiling an egg. I raised my hand and told her how wrong she was about how to boil an egg. Big mistake! She made me look up how to boil an egg. Then, I had to write 1000 times the entire instruction on boiling an egg. I never did like her after that!

CRAB STUFFED DEVILED EGGS

COOK TIME: 30 MINUTES | SERVES: 12

Ingredients

1 Dozen of eggs *(sliced in half, yoke removed, and saved in a bowl)*

2 Tablespoons of mayonnaise

2 Teaspoons of lemon juice

½ Tablespoon of grain mustard

2 Teaspoons of cayenne pepper

2 Teaspoons of old bay seasoning

2 Teaspoons of sugar

½ Cup of lump crab

Directions

Place 12 eggs into a pot. Cover with 5 or 6 inches of cold water. Sprinkle a half tablespoon of salt over the eggs. Bring the water to a boil and cook for about 15 minutes from the time the eggs began to boil. Pour of the water and run under cold water for about 10 minutes or until the eggs are cool enough to handle. In a large bowl, combine the ingredients and mix well. Taste and adjust the flavor to your likeness. Place the mixture into a pastry bag with a wide tip and pipe the filling into the egg. If you'd like a simple approach, use a tablespoon to place the mixture into the egg. Enjoy!

POTATOES ARE SUCH A WONDERFUL AND VERSATILE VEGETABLE. Over the years I've learned many ways to utilize this beautiful food. Potatoes take on whatever flavor you add to it. In addition to yielding its own individual flavor when eaten, thhere are over 4,500 different varieties of potatoes.

While I was working at Benvenue country club in Rocky Mount, North Carolina, I oversaw making the soups every morning. I'd have to come up with two different homemade soups per day. My all-time favorite was the potato & leek soup. The flavor, the creaminess, the fresh leeks, and the dry thyme all contribute to one marvelous soup.

POTATO & LEEK SOUP

COOK TIME: 25 MINUTES | SERVINGS VARY

Ingredients

1 Stick of salted butter

1 Large leek stalk *(thin sliced)*

1 White onion *(thin sliced)*

1 Pound of white potatoes *(peeled and diced)*

½ Gallon of chicken broth

2 Teaspoons of Kosher salt

1 Teaspoon of ground white pepper

1 Teaspoon of dry thyme

½ Cup of heavy cream

½ Cup of half and half

Directions

Place a skillet onto the stove on medium high. Add the butter and allow it to melt. Add the leeks and onion. Cover with a lid, reduce the heat to medium low and allow the onions to sweat. Cook for about 10 minutes.

In the meantime, place a gallon size pot onto the stove on high. Add the potatoes, chicken broth, and salt. Bring to a boil. Reduce the heat to medium. Add the pepper, salt, thyme, and leeks. Once the potatoes are fork tender, add the cream along with the half and half. Continue to cook for about 15 minutes. Taste and adjust flavors. If a thicker soup is desired; combine a half cup of all purpose flour with one cup of water. Mix until smooth and all lumps are gone. Bring the soup back up to a boil and stir in the flour mixture. Once the desired mixture is reached, turn off the stove and serve immediately.

MY VEGGIE LOVERS ARE GOING TO LOVE THIS. This recipe is quick, simple, and easy. I had recently contemplated becoming a vegan. Each year during the month of January I participate in the Danial fast. During the fast I only consume fruit, water, vegetables and water. After the fast I always feel like a new person, the therapeutic benefits are amazing. My breathing and sleep patterns even become better. However, I just can't seem to let go of meat.

GRILLED VEGETABLE & QUINOA SALAD

COOK TIMES VARY | SERVINGS VARY

Ingredients

VEGETABLE & QUINOA

12 Cups of vegetable broth

1 ½ Cups of quinoa *(rinsed)*

1 Large red bell pepper

½ Pound of broccoli crowns

½ Pound of cauliflower crowns

1 Pound of whole mushrooms *(white)*

1 Purple onion

4 Red potatoes *(sliced ¼ inch)*

2 Cups of chopped kale

SAUCE

1 Cup of red wine vinegar

½ Cup of honey

1 Bunch of sliced basil

2 Tablespoons of Dijon mustard

2 Tablespoons balsamic vinegar

¼ Cup of olive oil

Directions

Place a 2 ½ quart pot onto the stove. Prepare the quinoa according to the directions of the package. Substitute water for vegetable broth. Once the quinoa is prepared, spread onto a cookie sheet and place into the refrigerator to chill for later use. Prepare your grill to a good even cooking temp. Place the vegetables onto the grill. Grill for about 5 minutes. The potatoes should go a little longer until they are tender. In the meantime, combine all the ingredients of the dressing. Mix well. Add the quinoa, kale, and dressing. Mix well. Enjoy!

LOBSTER ENCHILADAS

COOK TIME: 45 MINUTES | SERVES: 4 - 6

Ingredients

2 Tablespoons of unsalted butter

1 Small onion (minced)

1 ½ Pound of chopped lobster (save the shells)

2 Cups of chicken broth

½ Cup of heavy cream

10 Flour tortillas

1 Cup of sour cream

2 Cups of queso blanco cheese (grated or shredded)

1 Cup of sharp cheddar

½ Cup of chopped cilantro

½ Cup of sliced jalapenos (optional)

Directions

PRE-HEAT THE OVEN TO 375. Place a skillet onto the stove on medium high. Place the butter, onion, and lobster into the skillet. Sautee the lobster for about three minutes. Turn off the stove and set the skillet aside to cool. Place a sauce pot onto the stove and add the chicken broth and lobster shells. Allow the broth to come to a boil. Reduce the heat and simmer for about 10 minutes. Remove all the shells from the broth. Add the heavy cream to the broth and continue to simmer for about five minutes more. On a clean surface lay out half the tortillas. Spread a thin layer of sour cream over each shell. Add the cheeses, and lobster equally divided on the shells. Roll each tortilla leaving the seam facing down. Repeat until remaining tortillas are used.

Spread a ½ cup of cream sauce evenly into a 13x9 baking dish. Place each enchilada into the dish with the seam facing down. Once the pan is full, top each enchilada with an additional cup of sauce. Top with remaining cheese, cilantro, and jalapenos. Bake for about 30 minutes. Enjoy!

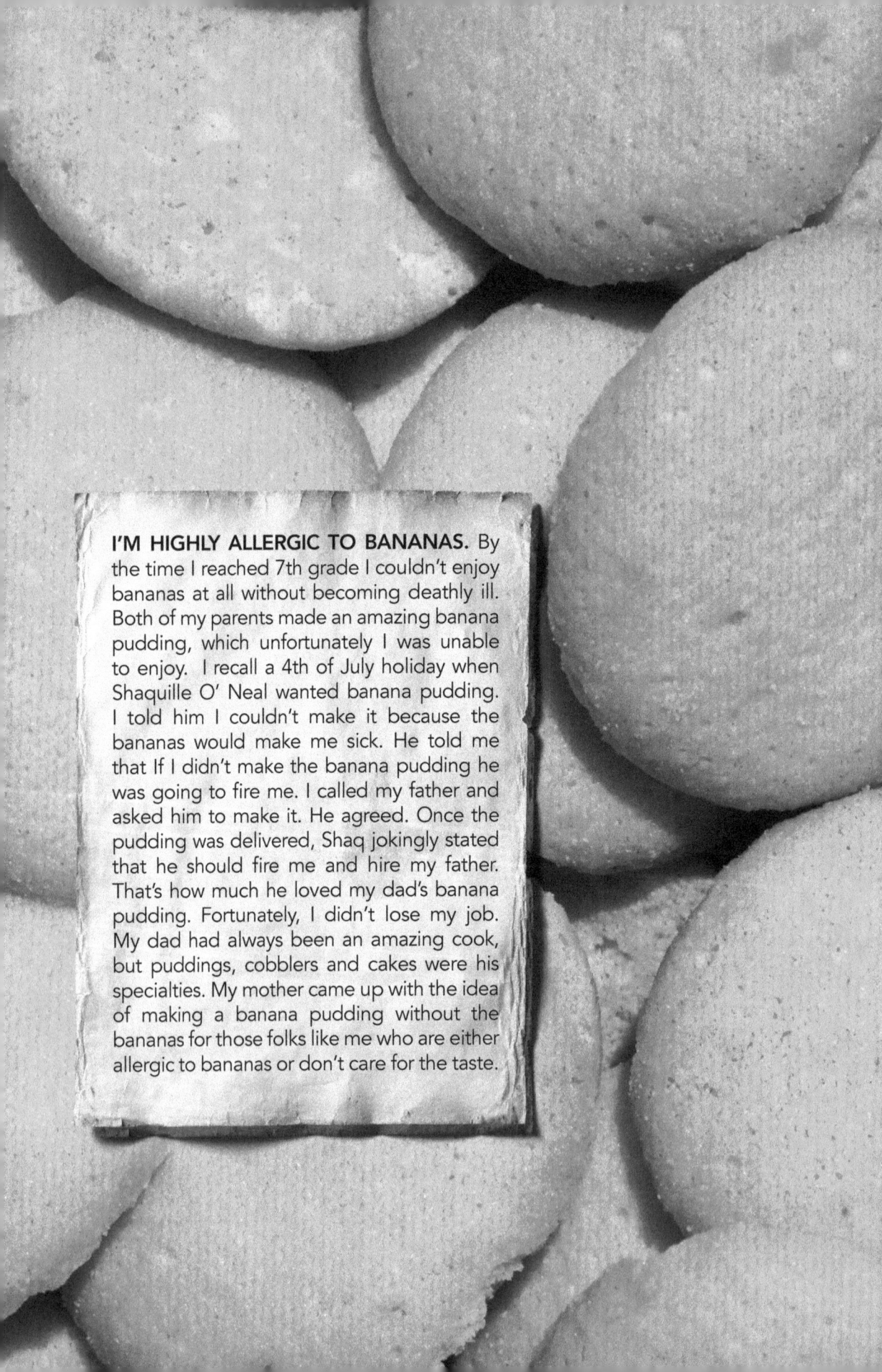

I'M HIGHLY ALLERGIC TO BANANAS. By the time I reached 7th grade I couldn't enjoy bananas at all without becoming deathly ill. Both of my parents made an amazing banana pudding, which unfortunately I was unable to enjoy. I recall a 4th of July holiday when Shaquille O' Neal wanted banana pudding. I told him I couldn't make it because the bananas would make me sick. He told me that If I didn't make the banana pudding he was going to fire me. I called my father and asked him to make it. He agreed. Once the pudding was delivered, Shaq jokingly stated that he should fire me and hire my father. That's how much he loved my dad's banana pudding. Fortunately, I didn't lose my job. My dad had always been an amazing cook, but puddings, cobblers and cakes were his specialties. My mother came up with the idea of making a banana pudding without the bananas for those folks like me who are either allergic to bananas or don't care for the taste.

BANANA LESS PUDDING

COOK TIME: 20 MINUTES | SERVES: 10

Ingredients

PUDDING

1 Cup of sugar

1/3 Cup of cornstarch

2 3/4 Cups of milk

½ Teaspoon of salt

6 Egg yolks, slightly beaten
(slightly beaten) (save all the whites)

2 Tablespoon of unsalted butter (melted)

2 Teaspoons of vanilla

1 Box of vanilla wafers

WHIPPED CREAM

2 Cups of heavy cream

½ Cup of powdered sugar

2 Teaspoons of vanilla extract

MERINGUE

Whites of 6 eggs

Pinch of salt

1/8 Teaspoon of cream of tartar

¼ Cup of sugar

NOTE: *Feel free to eat any remaining cookies, LOL! Leftover whipped cream can be placed into a plastic container or freezer bag and saved for about a month.*

Directions

PRE-HEAT THE OVEN TO 350. Place a large metal or glass mixing bowl into the freezer.

Place a large skillet on the stove on low heat. Add the sugar, cornstarch, milk, and salt to the skillet. Mix well. Continue stirring as the mix begins to thicken. Next, add the egg yolks; mix well. Once the mixture is thick, remove the skillet from the heat and allow to cool. Add the butter and vanilla. Mix well and set aside.

Remove the mixing bowl from the freezer. Pour the heavy cream into the bowl. Turn the mixer on high and continue to whip until the cream has stiff peaks. Turn off the mixer and add the powdered sugar and vanilla. Continue to whip for about another 10 seconds or so. Set aside.

Pour the egg whites and salt into another mixing bowl. Beat on low speed until frothy. Add the cream of tartar and increase the mixer speed to medium. The whites will become fluffy with large bubbles forming around the edges. Add the sugar a little at a time until all is incorporated. Continue to beat until stiff peaks form. Add the vanilla and turn off the mixer.

Place a large 13x9 glass baking dish onto the counter. Spoon a layer of pudding into the bottom of the dish. Place a layer of cookies over the pudding and then a layer of whipped cream. Repeat the steps in this order until the dish is full. Once the dish is full; Spoon the meringue over the top. Place into the oven to bake for about 12-15 minutes or until the meringue is browned. Remove the pudding from the oven and allow the pudding to cool. Place into the refrigerator to chill for about 4 hours. Enjoy!

WHO DOESN'T ENJOY A WONDERFUL MAC AND CHEESE RECIPE? My Aunt Bessie makes an incredible mac and cheese dish that we all look forward to during every family gathering. But, every now and then I like to switch it up and do some things differently. I was on the phone with my friend Deena one afternoon and she was sharing with me that she had just returned from dinner from one of Charlotte's top restaurants, JackBeagle's, which embodies the very essence of the Charlotte night life scene. So, I decided to put my own spin on this must sought after dish.

FIVE CHEESE & PORK BELLY MAC

COOK TIME: 35 MINUTES | SERVES: 8

Ingredients

2 Pounds of macaroni

1 Stick of salted butter

Seasoned salt to taste

Ground black pepper to taste

2 Cups of pulled or diced pork belly

1 Cup of sharp cheddar cheese

½ Cup of smoked gouda cheese

1 Cup of shredded pepper jack cheese

½ Cup of Gruyere cheese

4 Cans of condensed milk

1 Cups of half and half

Sliced Muenster cheese *(topping)*

Directions

PREHEAT THE OVEN TO 375. Boil the macaroni according to the directions on the package, then drain and rinse under cold water. Spray non-stick oil into a 13x9 casserole dish. Once the pasta is drained well, pour the macaroni into the dish. Slice the butter into pieces and scatter throughout the pasta. Season the pasta with seasoning salt and pepper. Add the cheddar, gouda, pepper jack, and gruyere cheese. Toss well. Add the milk along with the half and half. Mix well. Place into the oven and bake for about 20 minutes. Remove from the oven and mix well. Top with the muenster cheese. Return to the oven and continue cooking for an additional 15 minutes. Remove from the oven and let sit for about 10 minutes. Enjoy!

IT IS ALWAYS A THRILL WHEN TRAVELING THROUGH THE CAROLINAS BECAUSE YOU NEVER KNOW WHAT YOU MAY SEE. On a hot sunny day it's not an anomaly to see the workers in the fields as they plant and harvest cucumbers, peanuts, soy beans, corn, sweet potatoes, and tobacco. Around the holiday's most of the harvesting is already complete, the leftover sweet potatoes are sold off to the public or just left behind to be picked up by those driving by. My grandfather was the lover of anything sweet potato. I can't remember a day when I did not see sweet potatoes in my grandparent's kitchen.

MOMMA'S SWEET POTATO PIE

COOK TIME: 50 - 60 MINUTES | SERVINGS VARY

Ingredients

PIE CRUST

2 nine-inch pie pans

3 Cups of all-purpose flour

½ Teaspoon of salt

2 Sticks of unsalted butter

10 Tablespoons of ice cold water

BATTER

4 Medium size sweet potatoes

2 Sticks of butter

1 Cup of sugar

½ Cup of brown sugar

1 Teaspoon of nutmeg

1 Teaspoon of ground cinnamon

½ Tablespoon of vanilla extract

1 Can of condensed milk

2 Eggs

Directions

PRE-HEAT THE OVEN TO 375. To prepare the crust, combine the flour and salt. Mix well. Slice the butter into one-inch slices. Combine the butter with the flour and mix until the flour becomes coarse like the texture of cornmeal. Add the ice-cold water and mix with your hands until all the flour is incorporated. Place in the refrigerator for about an hour. Remove the dough from the refrigerator and set aside. Add a little flour to the counter. Place the dough on the flour. Add a little flour to the rolling pin. Roll the dough out to about a quarter of an inch thick. Carefully place the dough over the shell, and carefully mold into the shape of the shell. Trim off any extra dough. Prick the crust with a fork. Place the shells into the oven and bake for about 8 minutes.

Remove the crust from the oven and set aside to cool. In the meantime, place the sweet potatoes into a large mixing bowl. Mash the potatoes well. Add the remaining ingredients and mix well at a medium speed for about 5 minutes or until smooth. Divide the batter between the two crusts and bake for about 50-60 minutes. Remove from the oven and place on the counter and allow to cool before slicing.

That Salmon Recipe

My good friend Jesonya continues to refer to my SALMON DISH AS "THAT" SALMON RECIPE.

YOU EVER HAD SOMETHING SO GOOD BUT COULDN'T REMEMBER THE PROPER NAME OF IT? That's what happens whenever I prepare my grilled salmon recipe. My good friend Jesonya continues to refer to my salmon dish as "that" salmon recipe. Either way, it's a wonderful yet simple approach to cooking salmon that's just a little different than baking, poaching, or frying. The key to the success of this recipe is to not overcook it. When grilling salmon or any other fish, it's important to remove it from the grill just before it's done. Cover it with plastic wrap or foil and let it rest for a couple of minutes. You will end up with a juicy and delicious piece of fish.

"THAT" SALMON RECIPE

COOK TIME: 12 MINUTES | SERVES: 4 - 6

Ingredients

3 ½ - 4 Pound side of salmon *(skin on)*

½ Cup of Dijon mustard

2 Tablespoons of Tony's Creole seasoning

2 Teaspoons of ground coriander

1 Tablespoon of minced garlic

1 Teaspoon of coarse black pepper

2 Tablespoons of melted butter

Juice of ½ lemon

1 Tablespoon of fresh chopped rosemary

1 Tablespoon of fresh chopped thyme

Directions

Prepare the grill by first ensuring the grill is clean and coated with a lite coat of oil. In addition to that, I always use non-stick spray. Once the grill reaches about 300 degrees; Carefully place the fish onto the grill and close the top. This will ensure the fish gets that great smoky flavor to it. Cook the fish for about 12 minutes. Use two spatulas to carefully remove the salmon from the grill and place onto a platter. Cover with foil or plastic wrap until ready for serving.

> If you drink enough of it, *you just might find yourself* **MOWING THE LAWN,** even in the middle of the night.

WHAT'S A GREAT MEAL WITHOUT A GREAT DRINK? As I've traveled all over the world, I have had the privilege of traveling to many places and have met some wonderful people. But there's two things that often bring people together for sure. Great food and alcohol. I'm no mixologist. However, I've been known to put together some cool drinks. This drink along with its funny name have pleased many! I call it "mow the lawn," because the first time I made it, I said to myself, "it looks like somebody mowed the lawn." It's a very refreshing drink. It's a lady's drink. It can be as strong as you'd like with a little more vodka, or a little sweeter with a little more lemonade. If you drink enough of it, you just might find yourself mowing the lawn, even in the middle of the night. Shh!! Some things should be kept as a secret.

MOW THE LAWN

PREP TIME: 2 MINUTES | SERVINGS VARY

Ingredients

½ Liter of top shelf vodka

1 Quart of homemade lemonade

1 British cucumber *(sliced)*

1 Handful of mint *(stems included)*

10 Sprigs of fresh rosemary

2 Cups of simple syrup *(optional)*

Directions

Combine all the ingredients into your favorite glass pitcher and mix well. Add simple syrup for a sweeter result. Makes one pitcher.

I'M NO COFFEE DRINKER. All my friends know that about me. But, I do enjoy a cup of hot chocolate. I was at my apartment in Raleigh one day and decided I wanted to tinker with my hot chocolate. Not only did this warm me up but I slept like a baby.

ADULT HOT CHOCOLATE

PREP TIME: 7 MINUTES | SERVES: 6

Ingredients

¼ Cup of unsweetened cocoa powder

½ Cup of sugar

3 Teaspoons of vanilla

3 Tablespoons of Kahlua

½ Cup of Baileys Irish cream

1/3 Cup of Grand Marnier

3 Cups of milk

2/3 Cup of boiling water

Directions

Place a 2-quart pot onto the stove. Combine all the ingredients over medium high. Stir constantly to prevent scorching. Once the desired temperature is reached. Enjoy!

I CALL THIS DRINK MIMOSA ON STEROIDS. I came up with this drink while in Puerto Rico. One morning as we were preparing breakfast, I decided to do something different than just a regular mimosa The drinking glasses were sitting on the kitchen counter just as the sunlight hit the glass. It was the perfect breakfast drink. There's a little work involved with this one but it's well worth the effort and can be made ahead of time.

SUNNY LICKS

PREP TIME: **20** MINUTES | MAKES **6** DRINKS

Ingredients

8 Champagne flutes

4 Bartlett pears

2 Cinnamon sticks

1 Star anise

5 Apple cinnamon tea bags

4 Cups of pineapple juice

8 Cups of water

4 Cups of orange juice

½ Cup of rum

2 Cups of dry champagne

Fresh strawberries

Directions

Place a 5-quart pot onto the stove on medium high. Slice the pears in half length wise. Place the pears into the pot along with the cinnamon sticks, star anise, tea bags, pineapple juice, and water. Bring to a boil and reduce the heat to medium low. Once the pears are fork tender, remove the pear and tea bags from the pot. Stir in the orange juice and rum. Place the drink into the refrigerator until it gets cold. Fill each flute three quarters of the way full. Top with champagne and a fresh strawberry. (Makes 6 Drinks) Enjoy!

NOTE: I also like to sugar rim the glass first before filling. Use two saucers. Pour about a ¼ cup of orange juice onto one saucer and about a ½ cup of sugar onto the other. Tilt the rim of the glass to a 45-degree angle into the juice. Then, repeat the same step into the sugar.

> Gina says to me, *"You want a drink"* and of course I responded **"ABSOLUTELY."**

I LOVE ME SOME GINA NEELY. That's my friend and sister. She's so full of class and sassiness. I happened to travel to Memphis on business and just had to give her a call. So of course, Gina says to me, "You want a drink" and of course I responded "absolutely." I asked her what it was called, and she hit me with the show stopper. The "G" spot. Of course! Leave it to Gina to get the party started. She looked at me and said, "Get your mind out of the gutter!" This drink is amazing. It's her creation but I just had to borrow it!

THE "G" SPOT

PREP TIME: 2 MINUTES | SERVINGS: 4

Ingredients

2 Cups of Domaine de Canton French ginger liqueur

¾ Cup of Grand Marnier

4 ¼ Cups of Jose Cuervo golden margarita

Splash of orange juice in each glass

Directions

NOTE: Gina used a black sea salted rim. It made for a wonderful presentation. Enjoy!

I LOVE BREAKFAST POTATOES. My mother had a way of making breakfast a special event. To smell that sausage and biscuits or salmon croquettes cooking was incredible. Mom would always round out the meal with her delicious skillet potatoes. They were always cooked in a cast iron skillet. The delicious sweet onion cooked just right, with every carefully selected seasoning.

SKILLET POTATOES

COOK TIME: 35 MINUTES | SERVINGS: 10

Ingredients

2 Pounds of small white potatoes *(washed and all dirt removed)*

Pinch of table salt

2 Sticks of sweet cream butter

1 Yellow onion *(chopped)*

2 Teaspoons of dry thyme

1 Teaspoon of cayenne pepper

1 Tablespoon of garlic powder

2 Teaspoons of cracked black pepper

Pinch of sugar

2 Tablespoons of rotisserie seasoning

½ Tablespoon of seasoned salt

Directions

Place a pot onto the stove. Slice the potatoes about a ¼ inch thick and place into the pot and cover with cold water. Boil the potatoes until tender. Drain well. In the meantime, Place a large cast iron skillet onto the stove over medium high. Add the potatoes, butter, and onions. Mix well. Cover with a lid and reduce heat to medium low. Cook for about 5 minutes. Scrape the potatoes from the bottom. Add the remaining seasonings and gently mix well. Enjoy!

CARROT AND SWEET POTATO BISQUE ARE ONE OF MY FAVORITE SOUPS. I absolutely love the comfort food feeling I get during the winter when soups are in full consumption. This particular soup can be served hot or cold. There are a myriad of wonderful health benefits associated with both carrots and sweet potatoes. This soup is a source of natural energy, coupled with a balance of a sweet and savory taste is such an amazing treat! It's just right for those not so good days when you need a little extra comfort. Bon-appetite!'

CARROT AND SWEET POTATO BISQUE

COOK TIME: 25 MINUTES | SERVINGS: 4

Ingredients

½ Stick of unsalted butter

1 Vidalia onion *(chopped)*

½ Tablespoon of minced garlic

1 Teaspoon of Kosher salt

Cracked black pepper to taste

1 Jar of roasted red peppers

1 Quart of chicken broth

1 ½ Cup of apple juice

1 Large sweet potato *(peeled, and cubed)*

½ Pound of matchstick carrots

Pinch of nutmeg

¾ Cup of whipping cream

Directions

Place a large soup pot on the stove on medium high. Melt the butter. Add the onion, garlic, salt, pepper and roasted peppers. Sautee' the vegetables for about 4 minutes. Add the chicken broth, apple juice, sweet potatoes and carrots. Cover with a tight-fitting lid. Reduce the heat to medium low and cook for about 20 minutes or until the sweet potatoes are fork tender. Add the nutmeg and stir. Place the soup in a blender or use an immersion blender until smooth and free of lumps. Stir in the cream. Ladle the bisque into the bowl and serve immediately. Enjoy!

SOME DAYS I JUST FEEL LIKE I WANT A TASTE OF SOMETHING A LITTLE DIFFERENT FROM MY NORMAL FOOD CRAVINGS. I want something fun yet and simple, but beneficial to my health. It's like cheating on my diet but not quitting. I absolutely love kale, and I love, really love cheese. So why not put them together in a flaky yet buttery empanada? At least it's baked and not fried. This truly is a wonderful snack with a great source of iron and vitamin D. You can even pair it with your favorite sauce or salsa.

SMOKED GOUDA AND KALE EMPANADAS

COOK TIME: 20 - 25 MINUTES | SERVINGS: 12 EMPANADAS

Ingredients

2 Tablespoons of salted butter

3 Large hand full of fresh chopped kale

1 Large red bell pepper (chopped)

1 Shallot (chopped)

1 Tablespoon of garlic (chopped)

½ Cup of vegetable broth

1 Teaspoon of Kosher salt

½ Teaspoon of coarse black pepper

1 Egg

½ Cup of water

24 Small cubes of smoked gouda

12 Empanada rounds

1 Tablespoon of garlic powder

1 Tablespoon of cumin

Directions

PREHEAT THE OVEN TO 375. Place a large skillet on the stove over medium high. Add the butter to the skillet to melt. Add the kale, bell pepper, shallot, and garlic. Sautee for about 4 minutes. Add the broth, salt, and pepper. Continue to cook for an additional minute. Turn off the flame. Allow the filling to cool for handling. Drain any excess liquid. In a small bowl, whisk together the egg and water. Mix well. Using a pastry brush, apply the egg wash to the outer rim of the empanada rounds. Spoon about a tablespoon of filling and two gouda cubes over half the shell. Do not over stuff. Fold the round over, creating a half moon shape. Use a fork to press and seal the shell together. Spray a cookie sheet or half sheet pan with non-stick. Place the empanadas onto the pan. Lightly brush the egg wash over the empanadas. Combine the garlic powder and cumin. Mix well. Lightly sprinkle over the empanadas. Bake for about 20-25 minutes or until golden brown. Enjoy!

> *This blend of sweet and savory* delight has become one of **MY FAVORITE GO TO COOKING TECHNIQUES.**

SALMON IS TRULY ONE OF MY FAVORITE FISH. It's health benefits include omega-3 oil which is great for your joints, your skin, and many other health benefits. I've made this recipe countless times over the years. It's wonderful on a salad or as a main course. This blend of sweet and savory delight has become one of my favorite go to cooking techniques. It pairs well with rice and spinach for a great dose of iron and energy.

HONEY MUSTARD GLAZED SALMON

COOK TIME: 8 - 10 MINUTES | **SERVINGS:** 4

Ingredients

4 8oz. Fresh salmon fillets

4 Tablespoons of Dijon mustard

4 Tablespoons of honey

3 Teaspoons of minced garlic

1 Tablespoon of fresh chopped parsley

3 Tablespoons of extra virgin olive oil

Pinch of salt

12 Sprigs of fresh dill

Directions

PREHEAT THE OVEN TO 375. Place the salmon onto a sheet pan. Make sure the salmon isn't wet. If so, use a paper towel to pat dry. Doing this will cause the sauce to form a nice and even coating. In a mixing bowl, combine the mustard, honey, garlic, parsley, olive oil, and salt. Brush over the fish liberally. Bake for about 8-10 minutes. Remove from the oven and garnish with fresh dill. Enjoy!

THERE'S NOTHING LIKE A WONDERFULLY MADE SOUP. I believe that when a soup is made from the freshest of ingredients, the taste cannot be compared to anything else. One can only taste the love poured into every bowl. This soup is a spinoff of my favorite French style soup better known as Cassoulet or white bean stew. It's full of protein, good carbs, energy boosters, iron, and an overall great balance of flavor.

THE GREAT NORTHERN SOUP

COOK TIME: 35 MINUTES | SERVINGS: 10

Ingredients

¼ Cup of olive oil

½ Pound of ground turkey sausage

3 Boneless/skinless chicken breast *(bite size pieces)*

1 Yellow onion *(chopped)*

1 Teaspoon of dry thyme

2 Cups of diced Roma tomatoes

4 Cans of great northern beans *(do not drain)*

½ Tablespoon of seasoned salt

1 Teaspoon of coarse black pepper

Pinch of crushed red pepper flakes

½ Cup of white wine *(chardonnay)*

1 Cup of vegetable broth

2 Hand full of baby spinach

½ Cup of sour cream

Directions

Place a 5-quart pot onto the stove over medium high. Add the olive oil, sausage, and chicken. Sautee for about 5 minutes. Add the onion, thyme, and tomatoes. Stir well. Add the remaining ingredients and stir well. Reduce the heat to medium low. Continue to cook for about 30 minutes. Stir every five minutes or so to prevent sticking. Place an immersion blender into the pot and blend until the soup become smooth. Ladle the soup into a boul. Top with a dollop of sour cream. Serve with warm buttery bread and enjoy! Enjoy!

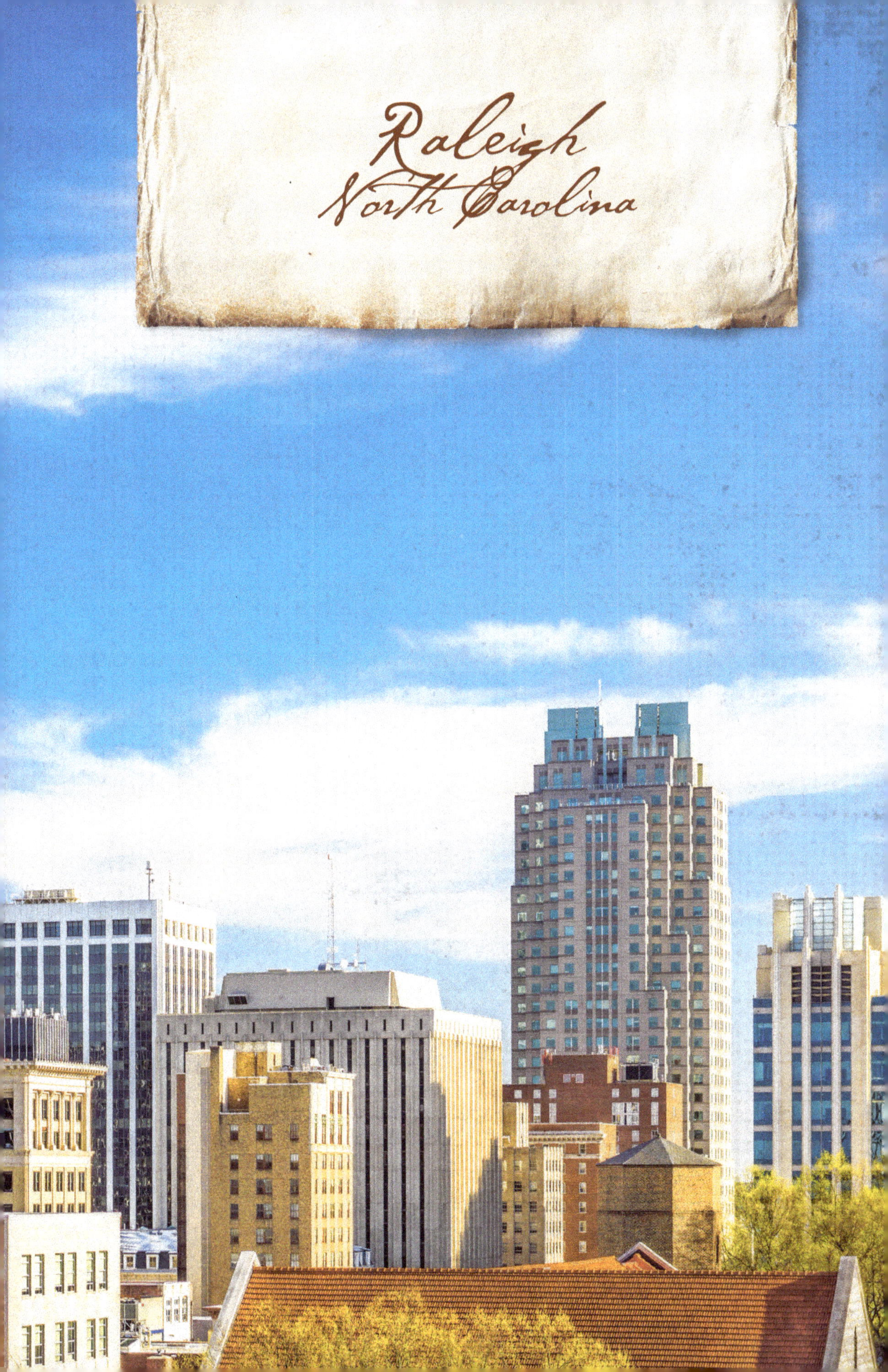
Raleigh
North Carolina

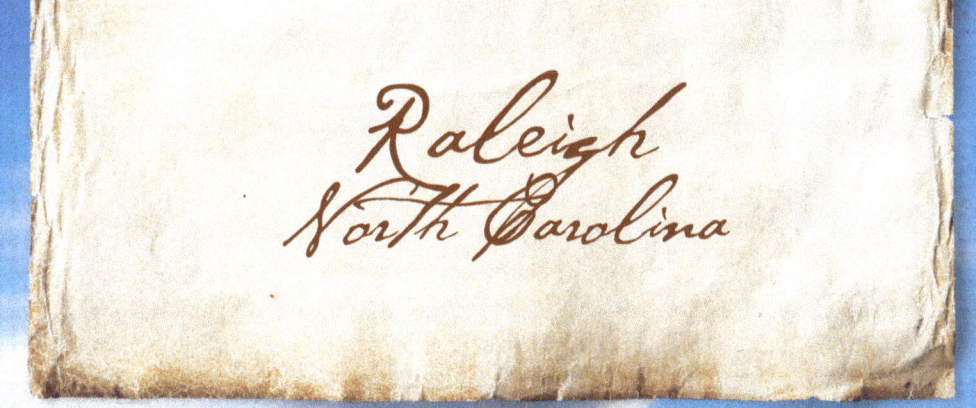

LIVER IS ONE OF THOSE PROTEINS WITH GREAT HEALTH BENEFITS. However, many people have ruined the taste by overcooking it. There's no other secret to liver other than to not overcook it. I borrowed this dish from my US Army days. The liver fiesta is a Spanish style dish that infuses a lot of wonderful flavors together. Not only is it a great dish full of protein, but it's also a good source of iron. When paired with wild rice, mashed potatoes or your favorite pasta, you incorporate an awesome source of energy. This truly is a well-balanced and an inexpensive meal.

SAUTÉED LIVER FIESTA

COOK TIME: 7 - 10 MINUTES | SERVINGS: 4

Ingredients

2 Cups of whole or low-fat milk

1 ½ - 2 Pounds of calf liver *(cut into finger width strips)*

2 Tablespoons of olive oil

2 Tablespoons of unsalted butter

½ Cup of all-purpose flour

1 Teaspoon of chili powder

1 Teaspoon of ground cumin

1 Teaspoon of garlic powder

1 Teaspoon of black pepper

2 Teaspoons of seasoned salt

3 Roma tomatoes *(diced)*

½ Cup of chicken broth

¼ Cup of white wine

1 Tablespoon of fresh chopped cilantro

Directions

Soak the liver in the milk for about two hours. Drain and set aside for later use. In a mixing bowl, combine the flour with the chili powder, cumin, garlic, black pepper, and season salt. Mix well. Place a cast iron skillet onto the stove over medium high. Add the olive oil and butter to the skillet. In the meantime, coat the liver into the flour mixture. Shake off the excess flour and place into the skillet. Sautee the liver for three minutes. Add the remaining ingredients and continue to cook for an additional 4 minutes. Serve over your favorite rice. Enjoy!

I ABSOLUTELY LOVE QUICHE. For me it's one of those anytime day or night meals. There's nothing like a flakey crust filled with fresh organic vegetables. In general quiche is also a great source of vitamin D, which is perfect for those who are vitamin D deficient. The many different varieties can range from just a couple of ingredients to whatever your imagination can come up with. To each his own I always say. This recipe can be made in a mini muffin pan or a variety of pie shell sizes. This combination is one of my all-time favorites. It's simple, quick and easy. After all, who has time to be in the kitchen all day unless you're a chef?

SPINACH AND CHEDDAR QUICHE

COOK TIME: 45 MINUTES | SERVINGS: 8

Ingredients

6 Large eggs *(beaten)*

1 ½ Cup of Cups of heavy cream

Salt and Pepper to taste

½ Teaspoon of dry thyme

1 Small yellow bell pepper *(small dice)*

1 Small red yellow bell pepper *(small dice)*

1 Small shallot *(minced)*

2 ½ Cups of fresh baby spinach

1 ½ Cups of shredded cheddar cheese

1 *(9 inch)* refrigerated pie crust

Directions

PREHEAT THE OVEN TO 375. Combine the eggs, cream, salt, and pepper, and thyme in a food processor or blender. Set aside. Place a small skillet onto the stove on medium high. Sautee the bell peppers, and shallots until softened. About 4 minutes. Add the spinach, and sautéed vegetables into a prepared pie crust. Pour the egg mixture into the crust. Bake for 40 minutes or until the egg mixture is set. Cool for about 10 minutes. Slice and enjoy!

HOW ABOUT A TASTE OF THE ISLANDS? I absolutely love fresh fruit. The natural sweetness of cooked fruit can't be compared to something processed and full of preservatives. If I'm going to add something sweet, I want to do it my way. I decided to have a little fun with this one. I added a little rum from the wonderful island of Puerto Rico.

DRUNKEN FRUIT COCKTAIL

COOK TIME: **8** MINUTES | SERVINGS: **4**

Ingredients

2 Coconut shells *(halved)*

½ Stick of Salted butter

½ Pint of fresh strawberries

1 Cup of fresh diced papaya

1 Cup of fresh diced pineapple

1 Granny smith apple *(peeled, seeds removed, diced)*

½ Cup of blueberries

½ Cup of blackberries

1 Cup of chopped walnuts *(optional)*

¼ Cup of brown sugar

½ Cup of sugar

1 Teaspoon of cinnamon

1 Teaspoon of vanilla

¼ Cup of Puerto Rican rum

4 Sprigs of fresh mint

Whipped cream *(optional)*

*Agave nectar (2 Tablespoons) or honey (1/2 cup) is a great substitute in place of the sugars

Directions

Place a large nonstick skillet onto the stove over medium high. Place the butter into the pan along with all the fruit and walnuts. Sautee for about 5 minutes. Add the sugars and allow the fruit to continue cooking until the sugars are dissolved and began to look like a sauce. Stir consistently to prevent sticking. Add the cinnamon and vanilla. Remove the skillet from the stove and pour in the rum. Once the rum is added, return the skillet to the flame. Use caution because the flame will ignite. Once the flame dies down, turn off the heat. Spoon the fruit into the halved coconut shells. Garnish with fresh mint and whipped cream. Enjoy!

Carolina Soul | 154

ONE OF THE THINGS I LOVE THE MOST ABOUT SMOOTHIES IS THE FACT THAT THE CHOICES ARE ENDLESS. Fruits and vegetables combined or individually is wonderful either way in a smoothie. The funny thing about this one, I can't taste it the way that I've described it. Why, you ask? I'm allergic to bananas. I'll leave it up to you to let me know how it turns out.

SMOOTHIE SUNRISE

PREP TIME: **1** MINUTES | SERVINGS: **2** CUPS

Ingredients

¼ Cup of frozen strawberries

¼ Cup of mango

½ Cup of orange juice

½ Banana

8 ounces of orange flavored yogurt

1 Tablespoon of agave nectar

Directions

Place all ingredients into a good blender. Mix on high for about 30 seconds. Pour into a container. Enjoy!

CARROT, APPLE AND **PEAR** SMOOTHIE

PREP TIME: 1 MINUTES | SERVINGS: 2 CUPS

Ingredients

½ Tray of white grape juice ice cubes *(prepare ahead of time)*

4 Carrots (peeled)

2 Red delicious apples

2 Asian pears

2 Tablespoons of honey

8 Ounces of orange flavored yogurt

Directions

Place all ingredients into a good blender. Mix on high for about 30 seconds. Pour into a container and go!

TROPICAL POPSICLE DELIGHT

PREP TIME: 1 MINUTES | SERVINGS: 10

Ingredients

1 Kiwi *(peeled and small diced)*

1 Cup of frozen or fresh strawberries

½ Cup of diced frozen mango

¼ Cup of white grape juice

2 Tablespoon of honey

Juice of ½ lemon

1 Pinch of sab

Directions

SPECIAL EQUIPMENT: 1 *(10 count)* 3-ounce ice pop mold. Combine all the ingredients into a blender and blend until smooth. Pour into the molds. Place in the freezer for at least 5 hours or overnight.

PINEAPPLE AND RUM? Sounds like a trip to the tropics. I love this wonderful combination. This wonderful buttery glaze is one that will speak loudly to the real meaning of sweet and meaty. I love this recipe and I'm sure you will as well.

PINEAPPLE RUM GLAZED CHICKEN BREAST

COOK TIME: **20** MINUTES | SERVINGS: **8**

Ingredients

8 Boneless skinless thin cut chickenbreast *(washed and drained well)*

½ Cup of all-purpose flour

Salt and Pepper to taste

2 Teaspoons of garlic powder

1 Teaspoon of fresh chopped tarragon

2 Tablespoons of unsalted butter

1 Tablespoon of olive oil

1 Cup of crushed pineapple and juice

2 Shots of Jamaican dark rum

Directions

Place a skillet on the stove over medium high. Combine the flour with salt, pepper and tarragon. Mix well. Season the chicken breast with the same seasonings as well. Add the butter and olive oil to the skillet. Coat the chicken in the flour mixture and carefully place into the skillet. Do not over crowd the pan. Sauté the breast until browned on both sides. Use a little more oil if necessary. Once all the breast is browned, add them back to the skillet and pour over the crushed pineapple and the juice as well. Cover with a lid or foil. Allow the chicken to cook for about 5 minutes. Remove the lid from the skillet. Remove the skillet from the burner and add the rum. Immediately return the skillet to the burner and reduce the heat to low. Continue cooking for about 12 minutes. Enjoy!

I LOVE OATMEAL. I always have. It's such a versatile food. Oatmeal is heart healthy, rich in fiber, calcium, and antioxidants, it also tastes great with sweet and savory foods. I love oatmeal with fruit. It served as the inspiration for this parfait. This is a wonderful high energy snack for anytime. It can also be used as a great meal replacement.

WILD BERRY PARFAIT TOPPED WITH HOMEMADE GRANOLA

COOK TIME: 30 MINUTES | SERVINGS: 4

Ingredients

1 Cup of old fashion oats

1 Tablespoon of chopped pecans

1 Tablespoon of brown sugar

Pinch of cinnamon

Pinch of nutmeg

Teaspoon of salt

1 ½ Tablespoon of honey

½ Tablespoon of vegetable oil

3 Cups of vanilla yogurt

1 Cup of frozen strawberries *(thawed)*

1 Pint of fresh raspberries, blueberries and blackberries

Directions

PREHEAT THE OVEN TO 300. Place a sheet of parchment paper on a cookie sheet. In a mixing bowl, add the oats, nuts, sugar, cinnamon, nutmeg, and salt. Mix well. Place a small sauce pot onto the stove on medium low. Add the honey and oil together and mix until smooth. Pour the liquid over the oat. Use a wooden spoon or spatula to mix well. Spread on the cookie sheet. Bake the granola until golden brown for about 35 minutes. Remove the pan from the oven and allow it to cool on a rack. Once the granola

Layer 1/3 cup of vanilla yogurt into the bottom of 4 glasses. Combine the strawberries and its liquids with the remaining berries. Alternate the fruit and granola with the yogurt until the glasses are filled. Enjoy!

QUINOA IS ONE OF THE MOST PROTEIN-RICH FOODS WE CAN EVER EAT. It has twice as much fiber as most grains and is gluten free. Paired with pinto beans, sweet potatoes and corn, this is a very high energy salad that is full of bold flavor that can be prepared ahead of time. The longer this salad sits the greater the flavors become.

SOUTHWESTERN QUINOA SALAD

COOK TIME: 30 MINUTES | SERVINGS: 8

Ingredients

QUINOA SALAD

2 Cups of quinoa *(rinsed)*

4 Cups of vegetable broth

1 ½ Cups of pinto beans *(cooked and chilled ahead of time)*

1 Large diced tomato

1 Large sweet potato *(small diced)*

1 Can of whole kernel corn

1 Jicama *(Peeled then small diced)*

1 Purple onion *(thinly sliced)*

CILANTRO LIME DRESSING

1 Cup of cilantro leaves

½ Cup of Greek yogurt

1 Tablespoon of minced garlic

Juice of 1 lime

1 Tablespoon of rotisserie seasoning

2 Teaspoons of smoked paprika

Pinch of salt

2 Tablespoons of cider vinegar

¼ Cup of olive oil

Directions

Combine the dressing ingredients in a blender. Blend for about 20 seconds. While the motor is still running, add the vinegar and olive oil. Refrigerate until ready for use. Prepare the quinoa per the directions on the package. Fluff with a fork. Spread the quinoa onto a pan and place into the refrigerator to cool. Place the sweet potato into a pot and add just enough water to cover. Bring to a boil and reduce to simmer. Cook until the potatoes are fork tender. Spread onto a cookie sheet, and put into the refrigerator until cold. In a large bowl, combine the quinoa, beans, tomato, sweet potato, corn, jicama, and onion. Mix well. Pour the desired amount of dressing into the salad. Toss well. Enjoy!

I CAN RECALL DOING A LIVE COOKING SHOW IN ALBANY, GEORGIA, THE "FOOD" FOR THE SHOW WAS AVOCADO. The benefits of avocados are amazing. It's such a versatile fruit. Avocados are great for your skin, damaged hair, has fiber, and more potassium than bananas. It's also heart healthy and has the ability to lower cholesterol and triglyceride levels. I paired this fruit with lump crab which is one of my favorite seafood items.

SPICY CRAB STUFFED AVOCADO

PREP TIME: 20 MINUTES | **SERVINGS:** 8

Ingredients

4 Ripe avocados *(sliced with pit removed) (Save the shells)*

½ Cup of lump crab

1 Small diced tomato

1 Teaspoon of Worcestershire sauce

1 Teaspoon of sugar

1 Teaspoon of tabasco sauce

2 Tablespoons of mayonnaise

1 Tablespoon of minced onion

½ Tablespoon of minced garlic

1 Tablespoon of lime juice

Salt and pepper to taste

2 Tablespoons of melted butter

¼ Cup of panko bread crumbs

Directions

Place a small skillet on the stove on medium high. Add the butter and bread crumbs to the pan and stir. Shift the pan around for about 30 seconds as the bread crumbs toast. Once the bread crumbs are golden brown remove the skillet from the stove and set aside to cool. Spoon the avocado into a mixing bowl. Use a spoon or fork to break up the avocado. Add the crab and remaining ingredients and mix well. Adjust flavor per your taste. Spoon the mixture back into the avocado shells. Garnish with bread crumb topping and cilantro. Enjoy!

I LOVE COOKING WITH FRUIT and *pairing it with unique items* to create a wonderful taste.

SOMETIMES A SIMPLE SALAD DRESSING IS EVERYTHING FOR A MEAL. I love cooking with fruit and pairing it with unique items to create a wonderful taste. Within this recipe, there is fiber, vitamin D, good carbs, omega-3 fatty acids, zinc, iron, and calcium. Now that's a dressing I can enjoy guilt free. This dressing can be stored for up to one week.

CREAMY APPLE & PEAR DRESSING

PREP TIME: 1 MINUTE | SERVINGS VARY

Ingredients

½ Cup of champagne vinegar

1 Cup of apple sauce

1 Asian or Bosc pear (diced)

2 Tablespoons of honey

Pinch of salt

¼ Cup of apple juice

¼ Cup of heavy cream

2 Teaspoons of walnut oil

Directions

Place in the blender everything except the oil. Combine for about 20 seconds. While the blender is still going, remove the lid and add the oil. Turn off the blender. Taste and adjust the flavors per your like. Pour over your salad or storage container. Refrigerate for up to three weeks.

CARROTS are *low in calories* and *high in nutrition.*

ONE OF MY FAVORITE VEGETABLES IS CARROTS. Over the years, I've discovered many useful ways to prepare this wonderful root vegetable. I was amazed when I discovered the fact that I had not been knowledgeable of all the different colors of carrots. They come in red, white, purple, yellow, and of course the orange. Carrots are low in calories and high in nutrition. One of the things I like to do when I cook carrots is sweeten them up a little.

SUNNY OJ POACHED CARROTS

COOK TIME: **10** MINUTES | SERVINGS: **4**

Ingredients

1 Cup of orange juice *(pulp optional)*

1 Cup of vegetable broth

4 Cloves

1 Tablespoon of vanilla

2 Tablespoons of brown sugar

1 Bay leaf

1 Pound of carrots *(peeled and cut into desired length and shape)*

½ Cup of marsala wine

Pinch of salt

Directions

Place a six-quart pot onto the stove on medium. Add the orange juice, broth, cloves, vanilla, brown sugar and bay leaf to the pot. Bring to a boil. Reduce the heat to simmer. Simmer for about 10 minutes. Enjoy!

Greenville
South Carolina

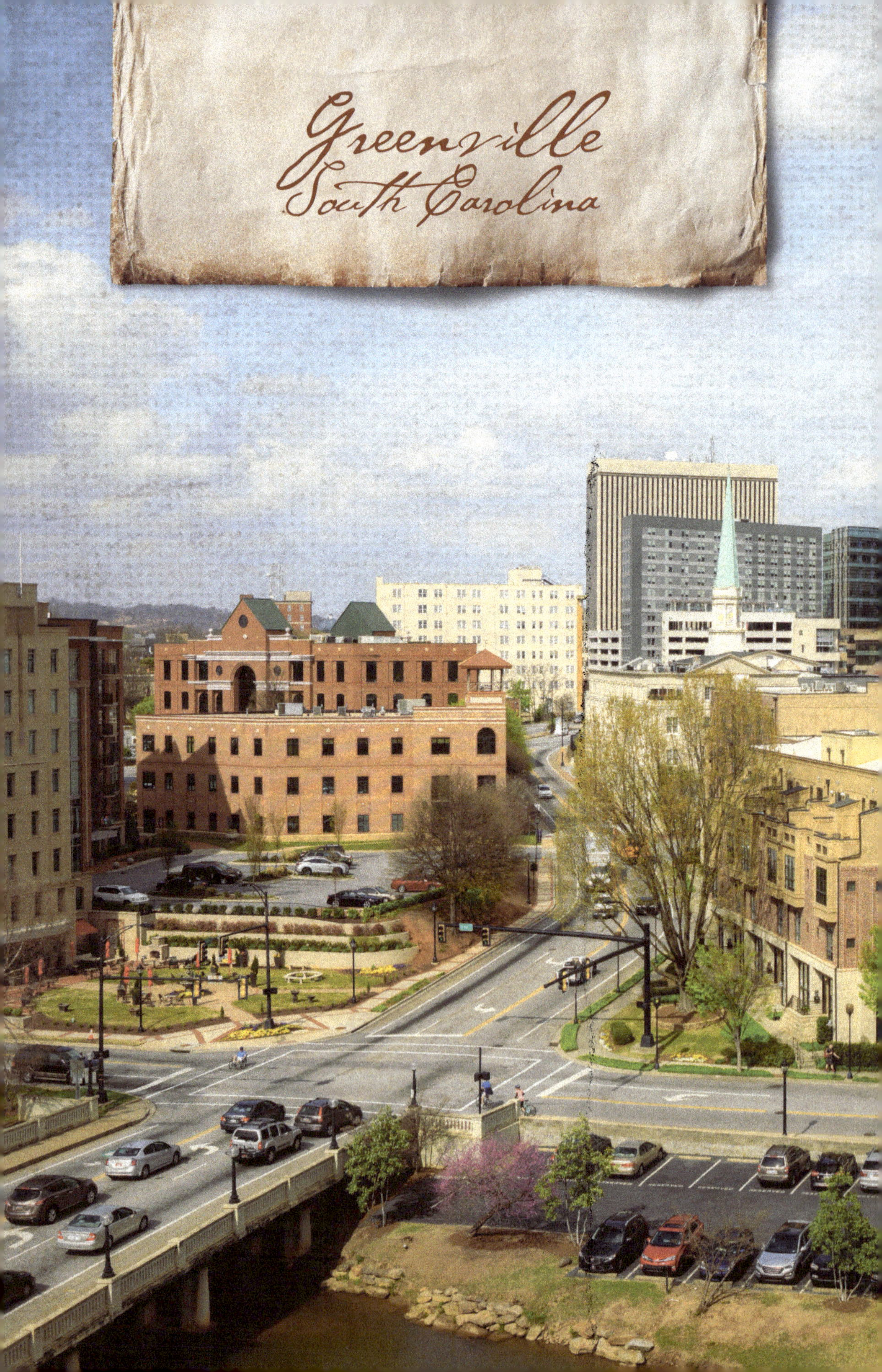

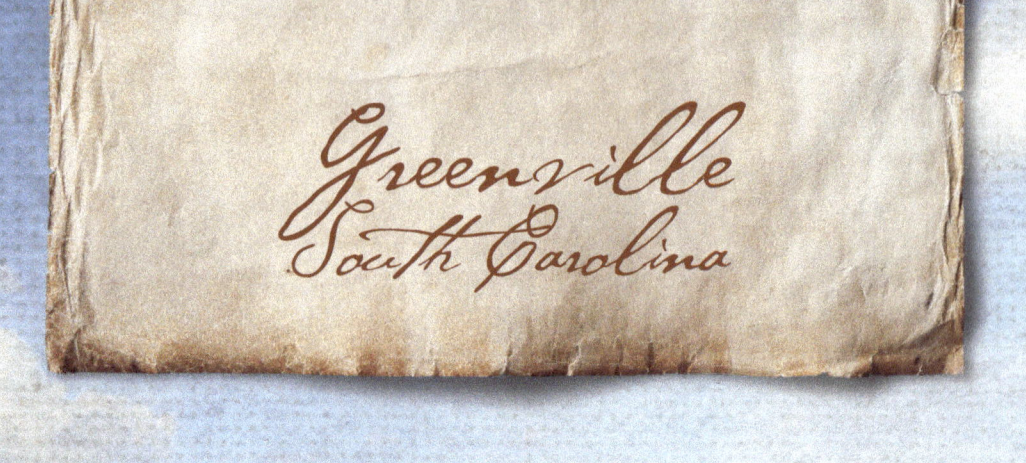

I REMEMBER WHEN I WAS YOUNGER MY AUNT BESSIE WOULD MAKE PEANUT BUTTER PIE. I'm a huge fan of peanut butter. In fact, one of my all-time favorite sandwiches is the famous PB&J. Every day when I came home from school, I would eat a sandwich. Sometimes, I'd eat two! Once she introduced me to the peanut butter pie, my world changed forever. If there's a need for something sweet for any sweet tooth people, I recommend this pie. It's quick, simple, and delicious. Eat up and enjoy. Cheers to Aunt Bessie for this one.

> If there's a need for something *sweet for any sweet tooth people,* **I RECOMMEND THIS PIE.**

CREAMY PEANUT BUTTER PIE

PREP TIME: 10 MINUTES | **SERVINGS:** 8

Ingredients

GRAHAM CRACKER CRUST

1 ½ Cups of graham cracker crumbs

1/3 Cup of white sugar

6 Tablespoons of melted butter

Pinch of cinnamon

FILLING

2 Tablespoons of sugar

1 Cup of heavy whipping cream

1 Cup of peanut butter

8 oz. of cream cheese

1 ¼ Cup of powdered sugar

¼ Cup of chopped peanuts

Directions

PRE-HEAT THE OVEN TO 350. Place a mixing bowl and beaters into the freezer for about 10 minutes. Combine the graham cracker crumbs, sugar, butter and cinnamon into a mixing bowl. Mix well. Press the mixture into a pie pan and bake until set. This will take about 7-8 minutes. In the meantime, remove the mixing bowl from the freezer. Pour in the sugar and heavy whipping cream. Whip on high until the cream forms and stiff peaks. Set aside. Whip the peanut butter and cream cheese together until smooth. Add the powdered sugar and chopped nuts. Spoon the whipped cream into the peanut butter mixture. Pour mixture into the graham cracker shell. Place into the refrigerator for at least an hour to set. Slice and enjoy with your favorite ice cream. Enjoy!

THE HEALTH BENEFITS OF THIS WONDERFUL ENCHILADA ARE OUTSTANDING. This dish is full of protein, fiber, good carbs, along with a freshness of bold flavors all combined to create an excellent experience for those who can do without the meat.

THREE BEAN ENCHILADAS

COOK TIME: **35** MINUTES | SERVINGS: **8**

Ingredients

1 Can of black beans
(rinsed and drained)

1 Can of kidney beans
(rinsed and drained)

1 Can of pinto beans
(rinsed and drained)

1 Can of whole kernel corn *(drained)*
(1 cup of frozen corn may be used)

½ Cup of fresh chopped cilantro
(may substitute with flat leaf parsley)

2 Cups of Spanish rice

½ Tablespoon of ground cumin

½ Tablespoon of garlic powder

1 Cup of sour cream

10 Large flour tortilla shells

2 Cups of shredded cheddar cheese

1 Can of enchilada sauce

GARNISH OPTIONS: Jalapeño peppers, cilantro, salsa, guacamole, diced tomatoes

Directions

PRE-HEAT THE OVEN TO 350. In a mixing bowl combine the beans, corn, cilantro, rice, cumin, and garlic. Mix well. Place the tortilla on a flat surface. Spoon just enough sour cream on the shell to cover. Next, place about three tablespoons of the filling onto the shell. Top with a tablespoon of cheese. Pour about a half cup of enchilada sauce into the casserole dish. Fold the tortilla and place into the casserole dish seam down. Repeat the steps until the dish is full. Pour the sauce over the top of the enchiladas. Top each one with about a tablespoon of cheese. Bake for about 35-40 minutes or until the enchiladas are golden brown and the cheese is melted. Garnish with your favorite toppings. Enjoy!

I CAN REMEMBER THE FIRST TIME I MADE THIS DISH. My cousin Fatimah was on a fast abstaining from all meat and sweets. She wanted something healthy and filling. I decided to put this recipe on Facebook. Apparently, everyone from Louisiana and abroad decided to remind me what a real gumbo is and that wasn't it. The backlash was very real. Fatimah made the gumbo and loved it. In addition to that, quite a few people made it as well. They in boxed me the results out of fear the Louisiana gumbo police would unleash the wrath onto them as well. This recipe is simply an alternative for those who may not want the meat or seafood. Either way, it was my recipe and I loved it. I hope you will as well.

VEGETARIAN GUMBO

COOK TIME: 30 MINUTES | SERVINGS: 10

Ingredients

4 Tablespoons of vegetable oil

4 Tablespoons of all-purpose flour

2 Medium tomatoes *(diced)*

2 Cups of chopped white onions

1 Tablespoons of chopped garlic

2 Tablespoons of tobasco sauce

2 Teaspoons of liquid smoke

Pinch of crushed red pepper flakes

1 Teaspoon of dry thyme

1 ½ Quart of vegetable stock or broth

1 Yellow, green, and red bell pepper *(diced)*

1 ½ Cup of diced celery

2 Zucchinis *(medium diced)*

2 Yellow squash *(medium diced)*

1 Cup each of Baby Bella and white mushrooms

1 Egg plant *(peeled and diced)*

1 ½ Cup of fresh sliced okra

4 Cups of Jasmine rice

½ Cup of fresh chopped parsley

Directions

Place a 5-quart pot with a heavy bottom on medium high. Add the oil and flour. Mix well constantly until the color becomes a rich brown. Do not walk away from the stove. The roux is the most important part of a gumbo.

Reduce the heat to low. Add the tomatoes, onions, garlic, tobasco, liquid smoke, thyme, and vegetable broth. Mix well. Simmer for about 15 minutes. Add the remaining vegetables. Cover and cook for about 30 minutes. Stir every 10 minutes or so from the bottom to prevent sticking. Add more vegetable broth for a lesser thickness. Serve with rice and garnish with fresh chopped parsley. Enjoy!

CREAM OF CHICKEN GUMBO CAME ABOUT BECAUSE OF A MISTAKE IN THE KITCHEN. It will go down in my personal history book as one of the greatest accidents that worked out for the best. I enjoy chicken and I absolutely love gumbo. What started out as salty became one of the most well-balanced dishes I ever created. I was torn between those who don't eat pork and those who don't eat shell fish. So, with that being the focal point of the challenge, I figured, let's make it feasible for both sides. Chicken it is!

CREAM OF CHICKEN GUMBO

COOK TIME: **30** MINUTES | SERVINGS: **10**

Ingredients

½ Cup of melted butter

½ Cup of all-purpose flour

2 Pounds of boneless skinless chicken breast or tenders

1 Yellow onion *(chopped)*

2 Teaspoons of old bay seasoning

1 Bay leaves

½ Cup of chopped parsley

2 Teaspoons of garlic powder

1 Tablespoon of rotisserie seasoning

2 Teaspoons of dry thyme

1 Tablespoon of coarse black pepper

½ Tablespoon of Kosher salt

1 Quart of chicken broth

1 Cups each of half and half, and heavy cream

2 Cups of sliced okra *(optional)*

1 Tablespoon of gumbo file'

1 Pot of wild rice

Directions

Place a 5-quart pot onto the stove over medium high. Add the butter, allow it to get hot but not burning. Add the flour and stir well until the roux becomes the light brown color of peanut butter. This will be a light roux instead of the usual dark roux. In a separate skillet add the chicken, onions. Sauté' until the chicken is almost done. Next, add the bay seasoning, garlic powder, rotisserie seasoning, thyme, pepper, salt. Continue cooking for about 5 minutes. Add the broth, allow the chicken to come to a boil. Mix well. Cover with a lid and reduce the heat to low. Cook for about 20 minutes. Add the half and half cream. Stir in while pouring. Bring the pot up to a simmer. Add the okra, cook for 4 minutes. Remove the gumbo from the burner. Stir in the file.' Add a half cup of rice to a bowl and ladle the gumbo around the rice. Serve immediately. Enjoy!

WHO DOESN'T LIKE A GOOD DEVILED EGG? I've come to enjoy all the wonderful different varieties of deviled eggs. The different varieties and flavors are endless. I wanted to add a simple spin on this well-known appetizer. It will surely be a hit at the next party.

SOUTHWESTERN CHICKEN DEVILED EGG

COOK TIME: 20 MINUTES | MAKES: 2 DOZEN

Ingredients

12 Eggs

1 Tablespoon of regular salt

1 Large boneless/skinless chicken breast

1 Teaspoon of season salt

½ Teaspoon of black pepper

1 Teaspoon of garlic powder

1 Teaspoon of ground cumin

2 Teaspoons of rotisserie seasoning

1 Tablespoon of olive oil

½ Cup of mayonnaise

½ Tablespoon of regular mustard

1 Tablespoon of lemon juice

1 Teaspoon of sugar

1 Teaspoon of tobasco sauce

Paprika or Cayenne pepper for garnish

Directions

Place 12 eggs into a pot. Add twice the amount of water to cover the eggs. Sprinkle the salt over the eggs. Bring the eggs to a boil. Boil for about 15-17 minutes. Remove the eggs from the stove and pour off the hot water. Run under cold water for about 10 minutes or until the eggs are cool and easy to handle. Carefully peel the eggs. Slice the eggs in half the long way. While the eggs are boiling, season the chicken with the season salt, black pepper, garlic powder, cumin and rotisserie seasoning. Place a skillet onto the stove on medium high. Add the olive oil and chicken to the pan. Sautee' the chicken for about 4 minutes on each side or until completely done. Remove the breast from the skillet and place into the refrigerator to cool. Once the chicken is cool, chop the chicken up into small pieces. In a mixing bowl, remove the yolk from the eggs and break up with a fork. Combine the chicken with the remaining ingredients. Mix well and taste. Adjust the seasoning. Use a pastry bag or a teaspoon to refill the eggs with the yolk mixture. Sprinkle with paprika or cayenne pepper. Enjoy!

AS A PERSONAL CHEF, THE DISH I PREPARED FOR MY VERY FIRST NBA CLIENT WAS SEAFOOD SPAGHETTI. I like the fact that the pasta options are interchangeable. I've found that angel hair and penne pasta works well with this dish also. The protein and good carbs will provide great energy for a day when you just might need a picker upper. This truly is one of my favorites.

SEAFOOD SPAGHETTI

COOK TIME: 30 MINUTES | SERVINGS: 8

Ingredients

1 Pound of spaghetti

1 Teaspoon of sea salt

2 Tablespoons of olive oil

½ Stick of unsalted butter

1 Pound of chicken sausage

Pinch of crushed red pepper flakes

2 Teaspoons of seafood seasonings

1 Tablespoon of chopped garlic

1 Small chopped shallot

1 Pound of Brussels sprouts *(sliced)*

2 Cups of chicken broth

¼ Cup of dry white wine

¼ Cup of pesto

1 ½ Pound of large shrimp *(size 16/20, peeled, deveined, tail removed)*

Parmesan cheese to taste

¼ Cup of chopped parsley

Directions

Place a 5-quart pot of water on the stove on high. Bring the water to a boil and add salt to the water. Add the spaghetti to the water and cook per the directions on the package. Once the pasta is cooked, drain and place into a strainer. Run cold water over the pasta to stop the cooking process. Set aside for later use. In the meantime, place a large skillet on the stove on medium high. Add the olive oil, butter, sausage, and pepper flakes. Cook the sausage for about 4 minutes. Add the seafood seasoning, garlic, shallot, Brussels sprouts, chicken broth, wine, and pesto. Reduce the heat to medium low. Cover, cook for about 5 minutes. Remove the lid and add the shrimp. Continue cooking for about 4 minutes or until the shrimp is done. Do not overcook the shrimp. Add the pasta into the broth and toss well. Top with parmesan cheese and chopped parsley. May be served with fresh baked French Bread.

Wakanda Forever

WHO KNEW THAT A KID FROM ANDERSON, SOUTH CAROLINA *(CHADWICK BOSEMAN)* WOULD GROW UP TO BE THE STAR IN ONE OF THE GREATEST MOVIES OF OUR DAY?

I'm still on a natural high from the Black Panther movie. Because I'd waited a few days until the crowds of people died down from the immediate rush into the theaters, I ended up sitting in the theater in Rocky Mount by myself. I was loving it and I felt like I owned the place. That was until a group of about five ladies came in just as the movie started. After hearing all the rave reviews and seeing the box office numbers rise by the minute, I felt a sense of pride as I walked out of the theater. Now if someone can tell me where I can get one of those cars Shuri was driving, that would really make my day.

Although I've yet to set foot on the continent of Africa, I believe that I cook with the soul of Africa. It is my roots. Therefore, this recipe is a nod to the success of the Black Panther movie and how it has inspired me. I've always wanted to visit all of Africa. In fact, as I have begun to look at experimenting with African herbs and spices, I've stumbled upon a very popular stew that accentuates the taste my soulful palate loves to enjoy. I will call it. . .

WAKANDA STEW
(AFRICAN PEANUT STEW)

COOK TIME: 1 HOUR AND 15 MINUTES | **SERVINGS:** 6 - 8

Ingredients

- 2 Pounds of boneless skinless chicken thighs
- 8 Chicken wings
- 4 Large chicken legs
- 4 Tablespoons of canola oil
- 3 Tablespoons of salted butter
- 1 Large yellow onion
- ½ Tablespoon of ground ginger
- 1 Tablespoon of coriander
- 4 Sprigs of fresh thyme
- 3 Pounds of sweet potatoes *(peeled and diced into bite size pieces)*
- 8 Roma tomatoes (diced)
- 1 Can of tomato puree
- 5 Cups of chicken broth
- 1 ¼ Cup of peanut butter
- 1 Cup of roasted peanuts *(chopped)*
- 2 Teaspoons of cayenne pepper
- ½ Tablespoon of black pepper
- ¼ Cup of chopped cilantro
- ¼ Cup of lime juice

Directions

Wash the chicken well under cold water. Place an 8-quart pot onto the stove over medium high. Drain the chicken well and pat dry with paper towels. Add the oil to the pot and allow the oil to heat up for about two minutes. Add the chicken to the pot and brown on all sides. Don't overcrowd the pot. Brown in batches if necessary.

Set the chicken aside in a bowl until the vegetables are sautéed. Add the butter to the pot. Once the butter is melted, add the onions, ginger, coriander, thyme, and sweet potatoes. Stir well to prevent sticking. Add the sweet potatoes and continue cooking for about three minutes. Add the diced tomatoes, tomato puree, and chicken broth. Mix well. Add the peanut butter, cayenne pepper, and black pepper. Bring to a boil. Cover with a tight-fitting lid and reduce the heat to low. Cook for about one hour and fifteen minutes. Remove the bones from the pot prior to serving. Stir in the cilantro and lime juice. Serve over white or coconut rice.

WHY STOP AT ONE WAKANDA RECIPE WHEN YOU CAN HAVE MORE? I wanted to add in a great recipe that's healthy and simple to make. Best of all, it won't keep you in the kitchen all day. I love rice and it's been a while since I've had a good rice pudding. South Africa is home to several phenomenal rice dishes. So once again, in the spirit of cooking with the soul of the south, this rice dish will surly please your sweet tooth of a palate.

WAKANDA RICE PUDDING
(BLACK RICE PUDDING)

COOK TIME: 45 MINUTES | SERVINGS: 4

Ingredients

2 ½ Cups of water

1 Cup of black rice

1 Cup of coconut milk

1 Vanilla bean pod *(split length wise)*

¼ Cup of golden raisins

1 Teaspoon of fresh grated nutmeg

1 Teaspoon of ground cardamom

1 Cinnamon stick

Zest of ½ lemon

½ Cup of sugar

Pinch of salt

Fresh mint leaves *(optional)*

Toasted almonds *(toasted)*

Directions

Place a saucepot onto the stove over medium high. Add the water, rice, coconut milk, vanilla bean, raisins, cinnamon stick, nutmeg, and cardamom. Bring to a boil. Reduce the heat to medium high. Add the zest and lemon juice. Stir every couple of minutes or so. Add extra water, ¼ cup of water at a time if the rice gets too dry. Cook for 45 minutes or until the rice is tender. Stir in the sugar and salt. Garnish with fresh mint and sliced almonds!

Carolina Soul
THE DOWN HOME TASTE OF THE CAROLINAS

www.ingramcontent.com/pod-product-compliance
Lightning Source LLC
Chambersburg PA
CBHW061208230426
43665CB00028B/2949